Mathematics

for the Common Core State Standards

ISBN 978-0-8454-6758-9

Table of Contents

Welcome to Finish Line Mathematics for the Common Core State Standards

About This Book

Finish Line Mathematics for the Common Core State Standards will help you get ready for math tests. You learn new math ideas each year. What you learn this year helps you in math class next year. This book helps you learn the most important ideas.

This book has units of lessons. Each lesson explains one main math idea. It uses examples. You have already learned these ideas in math class. The lesson helps you remember them.

Each lesson has practice problems. First are multiple-choice problems. Each problem has four answers. You must pick the best one. There is an example on this page. A box under the example explains the answer.

Next are short-answer problems. You have to write the answer to these problems. Sometimes you have to show your work. Sometimes you have to explain how you found your answer. There is another example on this page. The box underneath it tells you how to find the answer.

The last page has one or two long-answer problems. Each problem has two parts. You must write your answer to each part. Sometimes you must show your work. Sometimes you have to explain what you did. This item has a hint. It will help you think about the question.

Each unit has a review. You will do all three types of problems. You will use all the skills and ideas from the lesson.

A practice test is at the end of the book. The practice test has problems from the whole book. You will use all the math skills you practiced.

This book has a glossary. The glossary is a list of important math words. It tells you what the words mean. You can check here if you forget what a word means.

The Goals of Learning Math

Math is all around you. You use math every day. How can you become good at math?

First you need certain habits. A habit is the way you do something. You also need the right attitude. Attitude is the way you think about something.

- You read problems carefully. Then you plan what to do to find the answer. You do not give up. If your answer does not make sense, you try another way.
- You think about numbers using symbols. You think about something in real life using numbers and math signs.
- You come up with ideas about something. Then you give reasons to show why you are correct. You use what you know to give reasons. You think about other people's ideas. You decide if they make sense. You ask questions to help you understand.
- You use math models. You make drawings and graphs. You write number sentences to show a real-life problem. You decide if your model makes sense.
- You know how to use rulers and other math tools. You also know when to use them.
- You work carefully. You use the right symbols. You do your work correctly. You always label your answers. You use the best words to explain what you did.
- You build on what you know. You see how different parts of math work together. You use what you have already learned to understand a new idea.
- You look for patterns in math. Patterns can help you find shortcuts. You decide if your shortcut worked or not.

These habits help you learn new mathematical ideas. They help you remember and use the ideas. They also will make math easier to do. Then you can use math even more in your everyday life!

Unit 1

Number Sense

- **Lesson 1 Place Value** reviews how to identify the place value of digits in a three-digit number.
- **Lesson 2 Reading and Writing Numbers** reviews different ways to write whole numbers.
- **Lesson 3 Counting** reviews skip counting by 5's, 10's, and 100's.
- **Lesson 4 Comparing Numbers** reviews how to compare two numbers using the <, >, and = symbols.

LESSON 1

Place Value

2.NBT.1.a, b

There are 10 digits: 0, 1, 2, 3, 4, 5, 6, 7, 8, and 9.

Some numbers have one digit:

8 4 7

Some numbers have two digits:

34 90 61

Some numbers have three digits:

257 309 180

The ones place is always the farthest to the right. The tens place is to the left of the ones place. The hundreds place is to the left of the tens place.

The digit 0 is a **placeholder.** It shows that the value of a place is 0.

A number is made up of digits. Each **digit** has a value. The value depends on where the digit is in the number. This is called the **place value.**

This chart shows the number 495. What is the place value of each digit in this number?

Hundreds	Tens	Ones
4	9	5

The 4 is in the **hundreds** place. Its place value is 4 hundreds. The 9 is in the **tens** place. Its place value is 9 tens. The 5 is in the **ones** place. Its place value is 5 ones. The number 495 is the same as 4 hundreds, 9 tens, and 5 ones.

The value of each place is always ten times the value of the place to its right. Think of 1 hundred as 10 tens.

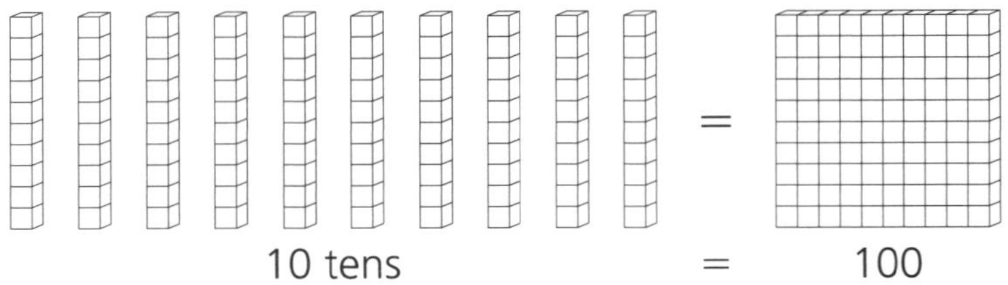

10 tens = 100

Some numbers have a 0 as a digit. This means that the value of that place is 0.

The number 800 has 8 hundreds, 0 tens, and 0 ones.
The number 305 has 3 hundreds, 0 tens, and 5 ones.
The number 640 has 6 hundreds, 4 tens, and 0 ones.

Read each problem. Circle the letter of the best answer.

SAMPLE What is the value of the 5 in 583?

A 5 B 50 C 500 D 5,000

The correct answer is C. The 5 is in the third place from the right. The first place is the ones place. The second place is the tens place. The third place is the hundreds place. The 5 is in the hundreds place. So the value of the 5 is 5 hundreds, or 500.

1 How many tens are in 100?

A 1
C 20
B 10
D 100

2 Which is the same as 900?

A 9 tens and 0 ones
B 9 tens and 0 tens
C 9 hundreds, 0 tens, and 1 one
D 9 hundreds, 0 tens, and 0 ones

3 Which number shows 4 hundreds, 9 tens, and 2 ones?

A 249
B 429
C 492
D 942

4 Which number has 0 tens?

A 590
C 83
B 302
D 40

5 What number does this model show?

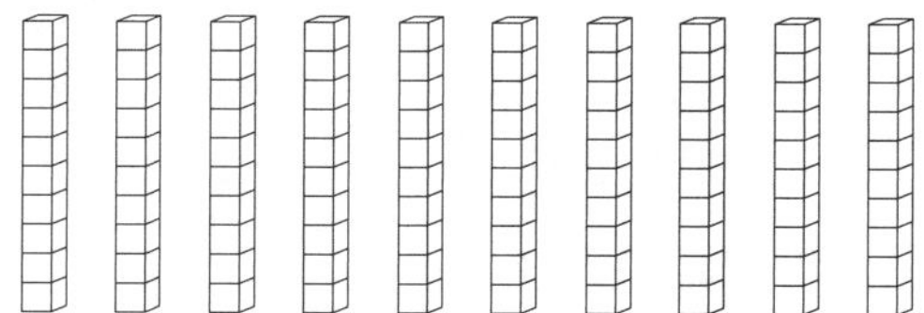

A 1
C 100
B 10
D 1,000

6 Which is the same as 2 hundreds, 0 tens, and 0 ones?

A 020
C 202
B 002
D 200

7 In which number does the 7 stand for 70?

A 700
B 370
C 287
D 167

Read each problem. Write your answer.

SAMPLE Kingda Ka is the tallest roller coaster in America. Its height is a three-digit number. It is measured in feet. The height has an 8 in the ones place. It has a 1 in the tens place. It has a 4 in the hundreds place. What is the height of Kingda Ka?

Answer ____________________

> **Kingda Ka is 418 feet high. A three-digit number has three places. The ones place is on the right. The tens place is to the left of the ones place. The hundreds place is to the left of the tens place. There is a 4 in the hundreds place. There is a 1 in the tens place. There is an 8 in the ones place. The number is 418.**

8 A path in a park is 675 feet long. What digit is in the ones place in this number?

Answer __________

9 A bag contains 10 marbles. Omar has 10 bags. How many marbles does Omar have?

Answer __________

10 How many hundreds, tens, and ones are in the number 600?

Answer ____

Read each problem. Write your answer to each part.

11 Paula built a tower using small building blocks. The number of blocks she used was a three-digit number. The number has 3 ones. It has 8 tens. It has 9 hundreds.

Part A How many building blocks did Paula use?

Answer ___________

Part B Explain how you found your answer.

Think about the order of the places in a three-digit number.

____

____

____

____

12 The first 500 people at a movie theater got free popcorn.

Part A How many hundreds, tens, and ones are in the number 500?

Hundreds ___________

Tens ___________

Ones ___________

Part B What do the 0's do in this number? Explain your answer.

____

____

Lesson 2

Reading and Writing Numbers

2.NBT.3

Whole numbers are the numbers you use to count and the number zero.

0 1 2 3 4 5 6...

These are whole numbers.

There are different ways to name whole numbers.

You can name a whole number in standard form.

6 25 987

You can name a whole number in word form.

six twenty-five nine hundred eighty-seven

You can name a whole number in expanded form. Write the value of each place in the number.

What is 25 in expanded form?

There are 2 tens, or 20. There are 5 ones, or 5.

$$25 = 20 + 5$$

What is 987 in expanded form?

There are 9 hundreds, or 900. There are 8 tens, or 80. There are 7 ones, or 7.

$$987 = 900 + 80 + 7$$

A number written as numerals is in **standard form.**

A number written as a sum of its place values is in **expanded form.**

A one-digit number is already in expanded form. It has a digit only in the ones place.

The ones place is the farthest place on the right. The tens place is to the left of the ones place. The hundreds place is to the left of the tens place.

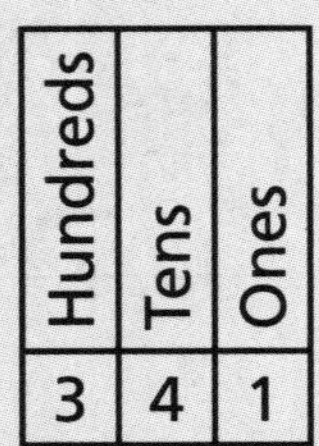

Hundreds	Tens	Ones
3	4	1

$300 + 40 + 1 = 341$

Read each problem. Circle the letter of the best answer.

SAMPLE Mike scored 653 points in a video game. What is 653 in word form?

A six five three

B six hundred fifty-three

C sixty fifty-three

D six hundred five three

The correct answer is B. The 6 is in the hundreds place. So the 6 is *six hundred.* There is a 5 in the tens place and a 3 in the ones place. These digits show *fifty-three.* So the number 653 is *six hundred fifty-three.*

1 There are eight hundred seventy-one people at a concert. What is another way to write this number?

A 871

B 817

C 718

D 87

2 Which shows 216 in expanded form?

A 2 + 1 + 6

B 20 + 10 + 60

C 200 + 10 + 6

D 200 + 100 + 60

3 Lacey had 14 new e-mails. What is this number written with words?

A one four

B ten four

C fourteen

D one hundred four

4 A scout troop sold 907 boxes of cookies. What is 907 written in expanded form?

A 900 + 7

B 9 + 0 + 7

C 900 + 10 + 7

D 900 + 700

5 Mrs. Carter wrote the number below in expanded form.

300 + 80 + 1

What is another way to write this number?

A 300801

B 381

C 318

D 183

Read each problem. Write your answer.

SAMPLE There were four hundred sixteen people on an airplane. Write four hundred sixteen in standard form.

Answer __________

Four hundred sixteen is written as 416 in standard form. Write each digit in the correct place. The number *four hundred sixteen* has a 4 in the hundreds place. The number *sixteen* has a 1 in the tens place and a 6 in the ones place. So the number is 416.

6 Aaron wrote the number 178 in expanded form. He wrote 1 + 7 + 8. Explain whether or not Aaron is correct.

____

____

____

7 Write the number 94 with words.

Answer ______________________________

8 A school cafeteria had 738 apples. How is 738 written in expanded form?

Answer ______________________________

Read each problem. Write your answer to each part.

9 A bookstore has 102 different magazines for sale.

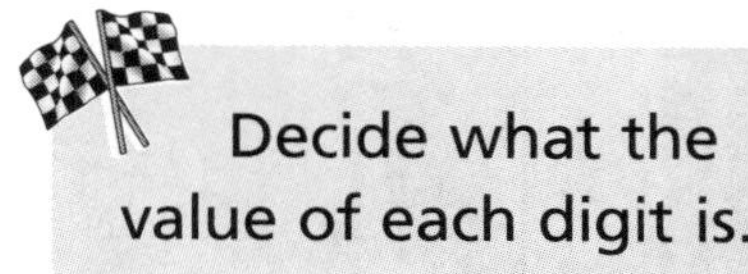

Part A What is 102 written in expanded form?

Answer ____________________

Part B Explain how you found your answer.

____

____

____

____

10 Look at the number below.

600 + 20 + 8

Part A What is this number written in standard form?

Answer __________

Part B What is this number written in word form?

Answer ____

Lesson 3

Counting

2.NBT.2

You can skip count by any number. Add the number to the last number you said. This is the next number.

When you skip count by 2's, add 2:

2, 4, 6, 8, 10, …

When you skip count by 5's, add 5:

5, 10, 15, 20, …

When you skip count by 100's, add 100:

50, 150, 250, 350, 450, …

You **count** with whole numbers.

0, 1, 2, 3, 4, 5, 6, 7, 8, 9, 10, 11, …, 100, …

You also use whole numbers to **skip count.** When you skip count, you say only some of the numbers.

Skip count by 5's: 5, 10, 15, 20, 25, …
Skip count by 10's: 10, 20, 30, 40, 50, …
Skip count by 100's: 100, 200, 300, 400, 500, …

A **number line** can help you skip count.

Skip count by 5's on this number line.

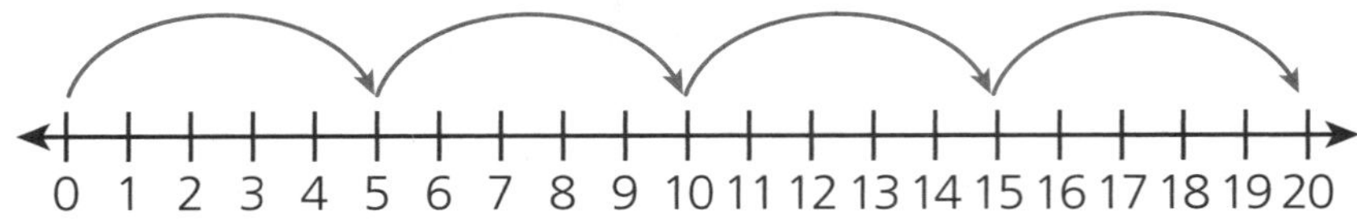

Start at 0. Count by 5's. Draw an arrow from one number to the next number you say.

A **number chart** can help you skip count.

This number chart shows skip counting by 10's.

1	2	3	4	5	6	7	8	9	10
11	12	13	14	15	16	17	18	19	20
21	22	23	24	25	26	27	28	29	30
31	32	33	34	35	36	37	38	39	40
41	42	43	44	45	46	47	48	49	50
51	52	53	54	55	56	57	58	59	60
61	62	63	64	65	66	67	68	69	70
71	72	73	74	75	76	77	78	79	80
81	82	83	84	85	86	87	88	89	90
91	92	93	94	95	96	97	98	99	100

Read each problem. Circle the letter of the best answer.

SAMPLE Lance is skip counting by 5's. Which of these groups of numbers will Lance say?

A 2, 4, 6, 8, …

B 3, 6, 9, 12, …

C 5, 10, 15, 20, …

D 5, 15, 25, 35, …

The correct answer is C. Lance is skip counting by 5's. So he will add 5 to each number he says to get the next number. First he says, "5." Then he adds 5 + 5 and says "10." Then he adds 10 + 5 and says "15." Next he adds 15 + 5 and says "20." So Lance says, "5, 10, 15, 20, …."

1 Rosa is skip counting. She counted 10, 20, 30, 40, 50. What will be the next number Rosa says?

A 55

B 60

C 70

D 100

2 Ian skip counted by 10's. He started with the number 8. What numbers will Ian say?

A 8, 10, 12, 14, …

B 8, 9, 10, 11, …

C 8, 10, 20, 30, …

D 8, 18, 28, 38, …

3 Heather says, "125, 225, 325, 425." How is Heather counting?

A by 1's

B by 5's

C by 10's

D by 100's

4 James is counting by 5's to 100. Which two numbers will he say?

A 65 and 80

B 55 and 72

C 34 and 48

D 100 and 200

5 Melissa is skip counting by 100's. She starts with 50. What is the next number she will say?

A 100

B 150

C 200

D 250

Read each problem. Write your answer.

SAMPLE Brent is skip counting. He says, "25, 35, 45, 55." How is Brent counting?

Answer ______________________

Brent is skip counting by 10's. He adds 10 to each number to get the next number: 25 + 10 = 35, 35 + 10 = 45, 45 + 10 = 55.

6 Vijay skip counted by 5's. He started at 40 and ended at 80. What numbers did Vijay say?

Answer ______________________

7 Mya skip counted from 0 to 50 by 5's. Her sister Jasmine skip counted from 0 to 50 by 10's. What numbers did both Mya and Jasmine say?

Answer ______________________

8 Parker wants to use this number line to show skip counting by 2's. Draw arrows on this number line to show skip counting by 2's.

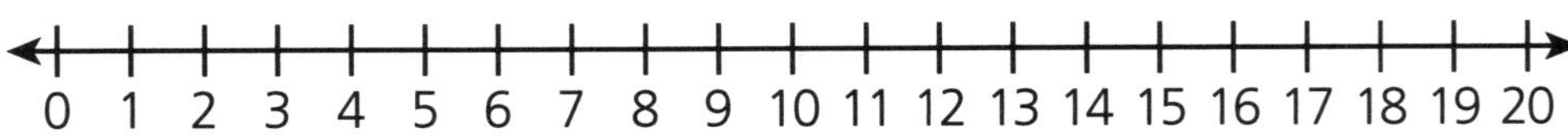

Read the problem. Write your answer to each part.

9 Look at this number chart.

1	2	3	4	5	6	7	8	9	10
11	12	13	14	15	16	17	18	19	20
21	22	23	24	25	26	27	28	29	30
31	32	33	34	35	36	37	38	39	40
41	42	43	44	45	46	47	48	49	50
51	52	53	54	55	56	57	58	59	60
61	62	63	64	65	66	67	68	69	70
71	72	73	74	75	76	77	78	79	80
81	82	83	84	85	86	87	88	89	90
91	92	93	94	95	96	97	98	99	100

Part A Katy says, "2, 12, 22, 32, 42." How is Katy counting?

How are the numbers that Katy says changing?

Answer ____________________

Part B Bill starts at 4. He skip counts by the same number that Katy skip counted by. What are the first five numbers that Bill will say? Explain how you know.

____

____

____

____

Lesson 4

Comparing Numbers

2.NBT.4

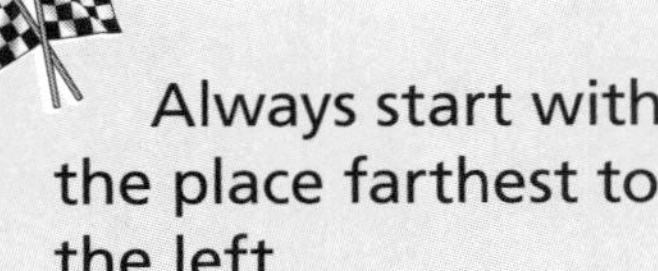

Always start with the place farthest to the left.

The symbols $<$ and $>$ always point to the smaller number.

$15 < 18$

$428 > 421$

You can **compare** two numbers. Decide which one is greater than or less than the other.

Compare numbers by looking at the digits in the same places. Start on the left.

Which number is greater?

474 or 472

First look at the hundreds digits.

474 **4**72

The hundreds digits are the same. Look at the tens digits.

4**7**4 4**7**2

The tens digits are the same. Look at the ones digits.

47**4** 47**2**

The ones digits are different. Compare the ones digits: 4 is greater than 2. So 474 is greater than 472.

You can use symbols to compare numbers.

The $>$ symbol means "is greater than."

$325 > 318$ means "325 is greater than 318."

The $<$ symbol means "is less than."

$561 < 575$ means "561 is less than 575."

The $=$ symbol means "is equal to."

$732 = 732$ means "732 is equal to 732."

Read each problem. Circle the letter of the best answer.

SAMPLE Which number sentence is true?

A $876 < 881$ **C** $907 > 970$

B $352 < 325$ **D** $194 > 199$

The correct answer is A. The symbol < means "is less than." The symbol > means "is greater than." Compare numbers by comparing the digits in the same place. In choice A, both numbers have an 8 in the hundreds place. Compare the tens: 7 tens are less than 8 tens. So 876 is less than 881, or $876 < 881$.

1 Which number is greater than 635?

A 605

B 630

C 638

D 356

2 Alison took 754 pictures on vacation. Joyce took 798 pictures. Which compares these numbers correctly?

A $754 > 798$

B $754 < 798$

C $798 < 754$

D $798 = 754$

3 There are 211 second graders. There are more third graders than second graders. How many third graders could there be?

A 198

B 201

C 211

D 215

4 Which symbol goes in the box to make this number sentence true?

$357 \square 342$

A $>$ **C** $+$

B $<$ **D** $=$

5 Which number is less than 983?

A 989 **C** 984

B 973 **D** 983

Read each problem. Write your answer.

SAMPLE Curt read two books in August. One book had 187 pages. The other book had 154 pages. Compare the number of pages in these books. Use the >, <, or = symbol.

Answer ____________________

The correct way to compare these numbers is 187 > 154, or 154 < 187. To compare two numbers, first look at the digit in the hundreds place. Both numbers have a 1 in the hundreds place. Look at the digits in the tens place. These digits are different. So compare the tens digits: 8 > 5, so 187 > 154. You can also write that 154 < 187 because 5 < 8. The > and < symbols always point to the smaller number.

6 Mr. Chang bought two packs of paper.

Which pack of paper has the most sheets in it?

220 sheets	180 sheets
Pack A	**Pack B**

Answer ____________________

7 Write two different ways to compare the numbers 753 and 729. Use the > and < symbols.

Answer ____

8 Look at the numbers below.

417 ☐ 407

What symbol goes in the box to correctly compare the numbers?

Answer __________

Read each problem. Write your answer to each part.

9 This sign is on a trail in a park.

Windy Overlook:	**584 yards**
Sunshine Falls:	**532 yards**

Part A Which place is closer to the sign?

Answer ______________________________

Part B Explain how you found your answer.

The numbers show the distances from the sign. The place that is closer has a shorter distance.

____

____

____

____

10 Zoe compared two numbers.

421 □ 428

Part A Which symbol should Zoe put in the box to make this number sentence true?

Answer __________

Part B Zoe added 7 to the number on the left. Now what symbol should go in the box to make the number sentence true? Explain how you know.

____

____

REVIEW

Number Sense

Read each problem. Circle the letter of the best answer.

1 What is the value of the 2 is 275?

A 2
B 20
C 200
D 2,000

2 Olivia says, "50, 55, 60, 65, 70." How is Olivia counting?

A by 2's
B by 5's
C by 10's
D by 100's

3 Juan wants to compare the numbers below.

637 □ 638

What symbol should Juan put in the box?

A =
B +
C >
D <

4 Which of the following is the same as 4 hundreds, 0 tens, and 0 ones?

A 400
B 410
C 004
D 40

5 What is another way to write 300 + 10 + 9?

A 913
B 193
C 319
D 30,109

6 How is 746 written in words?

A seven four six
B seven hundred forty-six
C seventy four six
D seven hundred four six

7 In which number does 1 stand for 100?

A 138
B 418
C 211
D 901

Read each problem. Write your answer.

8 Tina is skip counting by 10's. She starts at 500. She stops at 600. What numbers does Tina say?

Answer ______________________________

9 A board game has 278 red cards and 245 blue cards. Compare the number of red cards and the number of blue cards. Use the symbol >, <, or =.

Answer ____________________

10 Luke had 10 tens rods.

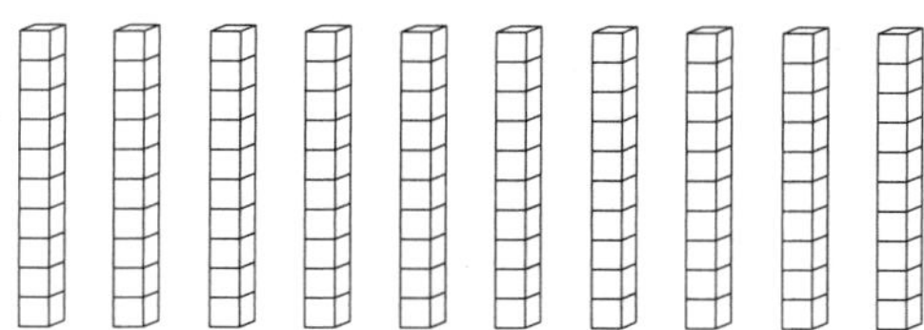

What number do Luke's tens rods show?

Answer __________

11 One day, a farmer picked three hundred ninety-eight apples. Write three hundred ninety-eight in standard form.

Answer __________

Read each problem. Write your answer to each part.

12 The Fisher family traveled 500 miles on vacation.

Part A How many hundreds, tens, and ones are in the number 500?

Hundreds __________

Tens __________

Ones __________

Part B What do the 0's do in the number 500? Explain how you know.

____

____

____

____

13 A candy store has 885 blue gumballs and 785 red gumballs.

Part A Use the > symbol to compare 885 and 785.

Answer ____________________

Part B Explain how you found your answer.

____

____

____

____

Unit 2

Addition

- **Lesson 1 Addition Basic Facts** reviews addition facts up to 20.
- **Lesson 2 Adding 10 and 100** reviews adding 10 and adding 100 to numbers.
- **Lesson 3 Adding Whole Numbers** reviews adding two- and three-digit numbers.
- **Lesson 4 Adding Whole Numbers with Regrouping** reviews adding two- and three-digit numbers when you have to regroup.
- **Lesson 5 Adding Equal Groups** reviews odd and even numbers and adding groups of equal size.

Lesson 1

Addition Basic Facts

2.OA.2

The **sum** is the answer in an addition problem.

2 + 3 = 5 ← Sum

A number added to itself is a **doubles fact.**

These are doubles facts:

1 + 1 = 2
2 + 2 = 4
3 + 3 = 6
4 + 4 = 8
5 + 5 = 10
6 + 6 = 12
7 + 7 = 14
8 + 8 = 16
9 + 9 = 18
10 + 10 = 20

Add to put numbers together. It is important to know the basic addition facts. Basic facts will help you to do many other math problems.

You can use different **strategies,** or ways to do something. Then you can do many addition problems in your head.

You can make ten to add.

Add: 8 + 4
Think: 4 = 2 + 2
Add: 8 + 2 = 10, 10 + 2 = 12
So, 8 + 4 = 12.

You can use doubles facts to add. Use doubles facts to help you find 1 more or 1 less.

Add: 6 + 7
Think: 6 + 6 + 1 = 12 + 1 = 13
So, 6 + 7 is 13.

Add: 6 + 5
Think: 6 + 6 − 1 = 12 − 1 = 11
So, 6 + 5 is 11.

You can count on to add.

Add: 5 + 2
Count on two more from 5: 6, 7
So, 5 + 2 = 7.

Read each problem. Circle the letter of the best answer.

SAMPLE What is the sum of 9 and 6?

A 6 **B** 9 **C** 15 **D** 16

The correct answer is C. The sum of 9 and 6 is 15. The word *sum* means the answer to an addition problem. So you will add 9 and 6. Think of a strategy that will help you add. Try to make 10. Think of 6 as 1 + 5. Think: 9 + 1 = 10, 10 + 5 = 15. So 9 + 6 = 15.

1 Add:

$3 + 3 = \square$

A 5 **C** 7

B 6 **D** 9

2 Ron wants to add 6 and 3 by counting on. What numbers will Ron say?

A 7, 8, 9

B 4, 5, 6

C 3, 4, 5, 6, 7, 8

D 1, 2, 3, 4, 5, 6, 7, 8, 9

3 Sarah wants to add 7 + 8. What doubles fact can she use to help her add?

A $5 + 5 = 10$

B $6 + 6 = 12$

C $7 + 7 = 14$

D $9 + 9 = 18$

4 Find the sum of 4 and 7.

A 14

B 13

C 12

D 11

5 Add:

$13 + 3 = \square$

A 10 **C** 15

B 13 **D** 16

6 Dion added 18 and 2 by counting on. What numbers did Dion say?

A 17, 16

B 18, 19

C 19, 20

D 17, 18, 19, 20

Read each problem. Write your answer.

SAMPLE What doubles fact could you use to add 8 + 9?

Answer ____________________

You could use the doubles fact 8 + 8 = 16. Then add 1 more: 8 + 8 + 1 = 16 + 1 = 17. Nine is 1 more than 8. So this doubles fact helps you add 8 + 9.

7 Ming will add 12 and 4 by counting on. What numbers will Ming say?

Answer ____________________

8 What is the sum of 5 and 8?

Answer __________

9 Explain how you can find the sum of 7 and 9 by making ten.

____

____

10 Add:

$$15 + 3 = \square$$

Answer __________

Read each problem. Write your answer to each part.

11 Ann wants to find the sum of 14 and 6 in her head.

Part A Explain what strategy Ann could use to add 14 and 6.

____

____

____

Look at the two numbers. One number is greater than 10. The numbers are not close to each other. What strategy is best for these two numbers?

Part B What is the sum of 14 and 6?

Answer __________

12 Mr. Ortiz wrote this addition problem on the board.

$$5 + 6 = \square$$

Part A Explain how you could find the sum using the make-ten strategy.

____

____

Part B Explain how you could find the sum using a doubles fact.

____

____

Lesson 2

Adding 10 and 100

2.NBT.8

The value of a digit depends on its place in a number.

Hundreds	Tens	Ones
4	9	5

To add tens, add the number of tens. Keep the number of ones the same.

28 + 10 = 38

To add hundreds, add the number of hundreds. Keep the ones and the tens the same.

285 + 100 = 385

You can use basic facts to help you add tens.

Add: 60 + 20
Think of 60 as 6 tens. Think of 20 as 2 tens.
6 tens + 2 tens = 8 tens
So, 60 + 20 = 80.

You can easily add tens in your head. Just add the number of tens in each number. The number of ones stays the same.

Add: 65 + 20
There are 6 tens in 65. Think of 20 as 2 tens.
Add: 6 tens + 2 tens = 8 tens
There are still 5 ones.
So, 65 + 20 = 85.

You can use basic facts to help you add hundreds.

Add: 600 + 200
Think of 600 as 6 hundreds. Think of 200 as 2 hundreds.
6 hundreds + 2 hundreds = 8 hundreds
So, 600 + 200 = 800.

You can easily add hundreds in your head. Just add the number of hundreds in each number. The number of ones and tens stay the same.

Add: 654 + 200
There are 6 hundreds in 654. Think of 200 as 2 hundreds.
Add: 6 hundreds + 2 hundreds = 8 hundreds
There are still 5 tens and 4 ones.
So, 654 + 200 = 854.

Read each problem. Circle the letter of the best answer.

SAMPLE What basic fact can you use to add 40 + 30?

A 4 + 4 = 8

B 4 + 3 = 7

C 5 + 2 = 7

D 3 + 3 = 6

You can use the basic fact 4 + 3 = 7 to add 40 + 30. Think of 40 as 4 tens. Think of 30 as 3 tens. Add the number of tens: 4 + 3 = 7. So 40 + 30 = 70.

1 Add:

10 + 80 = □

A 90

B 80

C 900

D 800

2 Nate used the basic fact 7 + 2 = 9 to solve an addition problem. Which addition problem could Nate have solved?

A 70 + 2 = □

B 90 + 20 = □

C 70 + 20 = □

D 700 + 20 = □

3 Add:

394 + 200 = □

A 500

B 594

C 600

D 694

4 What basic fact can you use to add 100 + 400?

A 2 + 3 = 5

B 1 + 3 = 4

C 2 + 1 = 3

D 1 + 4 = 5

5 Gigi has 6 boxes with 10 pencils in each box. She buys 1 more box with 10 pencils. How many pencils does she have in all?

A 6

B 60

C 7

D 70

6 Add:

670 + 300 = □

A 970

B 973

C 900

D 673

Read each problem. Write your answer.

SAMPLE A bakery sold 500 chocolate cookies. It sold 400 peanut butter cookies. How many cookies did the bakery sell in all?

Answer __________

The bakery sold 900 cookies in all. You must add hundreds. You can use basic facts to add hundreds. Think of 500 as 5 hundreds. Think of 400 as 4 hundreds. Use the basic fact 5 + 4 = 9. So 500 + 400 = 900.

7 What basic addition fact can you use to help you add 823 + 200?

Answer ____________________

8 Explain how you can use a basic addition fact to help you find the sum of 457 + 400.

____

____

____

9 Add:

$$50 + 30 = \square$$

Answer __________

Read each problem. Write your answer to each part.

10 Hyo planted 50 pumpkin seeds. He planted 50 corn seeds.

Think of 50 as a number of tens.

Part A How many seeds did Hyo plant in all?

Answer __________

Part B Explain how you found your answer.

____

____

____

____

11 A florist has 649 roses. She has 300 daisies.

Part A What basic fact can you use to help you add 649 and 300?

Answer ____________________

Part B How many roses and daisies does the florist have in all? Explain how you found your answer.

____

____

____

____

Lesson 3

Adding Whole Numbers

2.NBT.5, 2.NBT.6, 2.NBT.7, 2.NBT.9

You add to put numbers together.

The sum is the answer to an addition problem.

Always add from right to left.

Hundreds Ones
↓ ↓
567
↑
Tens

You can add numbers in any order. The sum is always the same.

3 + 4 = 7
4 + 3 = 7

1 + 2 + 3 = 3 + 3 = 6
3 + 2 + 1 = 5 + 1 = 6

You can add 0 to any number. The number stays the same.

5 + 0 = 5

0 + 746 = 746

Models can help you add.

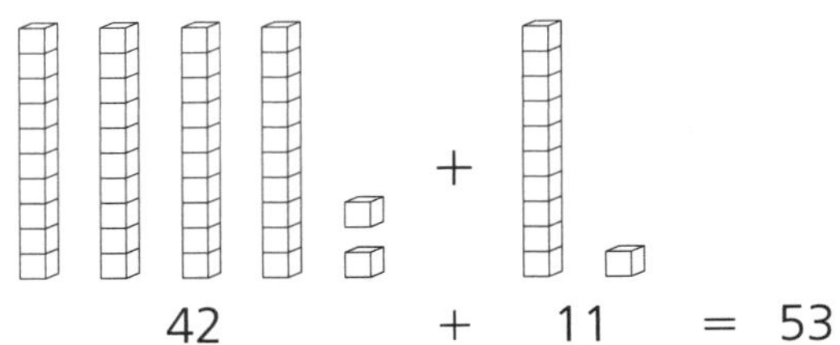

42 + 11 = 53

Add numbers by adding the digits in the same places.

Add: 75 + 22

Add the ones.	Add the tens.
75 +22 7	75 +22 97

So, 75 + 22 is 97.

Add: 512 + 235

Add the ones.	Add the tens.	Add the hundreds.
512 +235 7	512 +235 47	512 +235 747

So, 512 + 235 is 747.

You can add more than two numbers at a time.

Yuri had 21 balloon stickers, 33 sports stickers, and 32 flower stickers. How many stickers did Yuri have in all?

Add: 21 + 33 + 32
First add all the ones: 1 + 3 + 2 = 6
Then add all the tens: 2 + 3 + 3 = 8

Yuri had 86 stickers in all.

Read each problem. Circle the letter of the best answer.

SAMPLE Look at the model below.

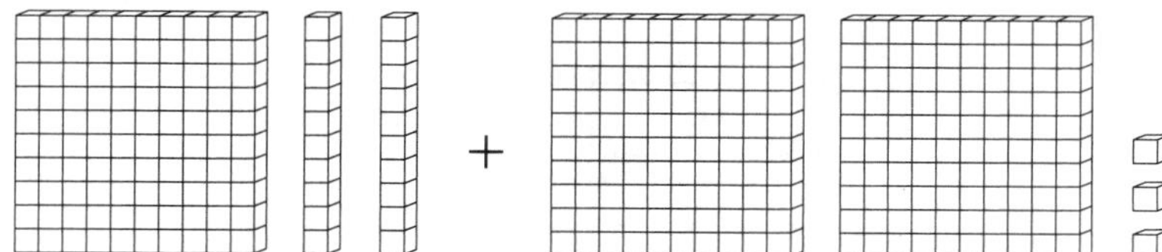

What sum does this model show?

A 143 B 223 C 303 D 323

The correct answer is D. This model shows 323. The first model shows 1 hundreds block and 2 tens rods. So it shows 120. The second model shows 2 hundreds blocks and 3 ones blocks. So it shows 203. Add: 120 + 203 = 323.

1 What is the sum of 51 and 18?

A 59 C 69

B 68 D 78

2 On Monday, Krista did 30 math problems. On Tuesday, she did 15 math problems. On Wednesday, she did 33 math problems. How many math problems did Krista do in all?

A 48 C 69

B 68 D 78

3 Add:

$$\begin{array}{r} 457 \\ +211 \\ \hline \end{array}$$

A 657 C 757

B 668 D 768

4 Enrico found 263 seashells. His sister found 324 seashells. How many seashells did they find in all?

A 477 C 577

B 487 D 587

5 Mrs. Garcia bought 56 green lollipops. She bought 33 red lollipops. How many lollipops did Mrs. Garcia buy in all?

A 59 C 89

B 86 D 99

6 Add:

$$\begin{array}{r} 24 \\ 21 \\ +14 \\ \hline \end{array}$$

A 58 C 68

B 59 D 69

Read each problem. Write your answer.

SAMPLE The table below shows the number of second graders in each class.

Class	Number
2-A	21
2-B	24
2-C	23

How many second graders are there in all?

Answer ___________

There are 68 second graders in all. Add the three numbers: 21 + 24 + 23. First add the ones: 1 + 4 + 3 = 5 + 3 = 8. Then add the tens: 2 + 2 + 2 = 4 + 2 = 6. So 21 + 24 + 23 = 68.

7 Mandi used base ten blocks to show the addition problem below.

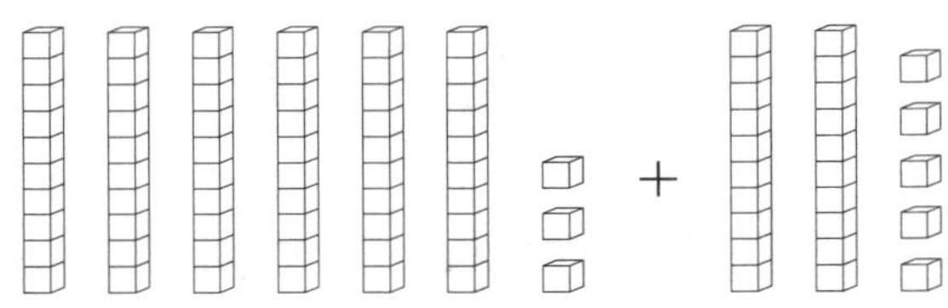

What is the sum of Mandi's addition problem?

Answer ___________

8 Find the sum. Show your work.

$$\begin{array}{r} 43 \\ +11 \\ \hline \end{array}$$

Answer ___________

Read each problem. Write your answer to each part.

9 Becky wants to find the sum of 17 and 61.

Part A What is the sum of 17 and 61?

Answer __________

Part B Explain how Becky could use base ten blocks to help her find the sum of 17 and 61.

How do base ten blocks show numbers?

____

____

____

____

10 Taylor and Faith are adding numbers. Taylor added 548 + 421.

Part A What is the sum of Taylor's problem?

Answer __________

Part B Faith added 421 + 548. Explain why she found the same sum as Taylor.

____

____

____

Lesson 4

Adding Whole Numbers with Regrouping

2.NBT.5, 2.NBT.6, 2.NBT.7, 2.NBT.9

The sum is the answer to an addition problem.

$2 + 2 = 4$
↑
Sum

Regroup 10 ones as 1 ten.

Regroup 10 tens as 1 hundred.

You can group numbers to add in any order. The sum will be the same.

$(6 + 4) + 9 = 10 + 9 = 19$

$6 + (4 + 9) = 6 + 13 = 19$

Add to find how many in all. **Regroup** when the sum of the digits in a place is 10 or more.

Add the digits in the same places. Add from right to left. Regroup from right to left.

Find the sum of 273 and 168.

$$\begin{array}{r} {}^{1} \\ 273 \\ +168 \\ \hline 1 \end{array}$$

Add the ones: 3 + 8 = 11 ones
Regroup 11 ones as 1 ten and 1 one.
Write 1 one in the ones place.
Then write 1 ten over the tens place.

$$\begin{array}{r} {}^{1\,1} \\ 273 \\ +168 \\ \hline 41 \end{array}$$

Add the tens: 1 + 7 + 6 = 14
Regroup 14 tens as 1 hundred and 4 tens.
Write 4 tens in the tens place.
Then write 1 hundred over the hundreds place.

$$\begin{array}{r} {}^{1\,1} \\ 273 \\ +168 \\ \hline 441 \end{array}$$

Add the hundreds: 1 + 2 + 1 = 4 hundreds
Write 4 hundreds in the hundreds place.

The sum of 273 and 168 is 441.

Read each problem. Circle the letter of the best answer.

SAMPLE Find the sum.

$$\begin{array}{r} 31 \\ 18 \\ 22 \\ +15 \\ \hline \end{array}$$

A 75 B 76 C 85 D 86

The correct answer is D. First add the ones: 1 + 8 + 2 + 5 = 16 ones. Regroup 16 ones as 1 ten and 6 ones. Write the 6 in the ones place. Write the 1 over the tens place. Then add the tens: 1 + 3 + 1 + 2 + 1 = 8 tens. So the sum is 86.

1 There are 484 children at a basketball game. There are 465 adults at the game. How many people are at the game in all?

A 849 C 949

B 859 D 959

2 Add:

$$\begin{array}{r} 74 \\ +96 \\ \hline \end{array}$$

A 179 C 169

B 170 D 160

3 Matt scored 357 points in a video game. Uma scored 281 points in the game. What was the total score?

A 638 C 648

B 639 D 649

4 The table below shows the number of boxes of cookies Kara sold on three days.

BOXES OF COOKIES SOLD

Day	Number
Monday	26
Tuesday	34
Wednesday	19

How many boxes of cookies did Kara sell in all?

A 69 C 79

B 70 D 80

5 Find the sum.

$$\begin{array}{r} 37 \\ +25 \\ \hline \end{array}$$

A 51 C 61

B 52 D 62

Read each problem. Write your answer.

SAMPLE A nature book showed 189 types of insects. It showed 392 types of birds. What was the total number of insects and birds in the book?

Answer ___________

The book showed 581 types of birds and insects. Add to find the total. First add the ones: 9 + 2 = 11 ones. Regroup 11 ones as 1 ten and 1 one. Add the tens: 1 + 8 + 9 = 18 tens. Regroup 18 tens as 1 hundred and 8 tens. Add the hundreds: 1 + 1 + 3 = 5 hundreds. There are 5 hundreds, 8 tens, and 1 one. So the total is 581.

6 Stacey added 16 + 18 and then added 22 to the sum. Wayne added 18 + 22 and then added 16 to the sum. Explain what is true about each sum.

____

____

7 There were 45 people on bus A. There were 48 people on bus B. How many people were on both buses?

Answer ___________

8 Angel weighs 35 pounds. Her brother Miguel weighs 86 pounds. Her sister Maria weighs 62 pounds. What is the total weight of Angel, Miguel, and Maria?

Answer ______________________

Read the problem. Write your answer to each part.

9 A baseball stadium is divided into sections. There are 276 people sitting in section 10. There are 329 people sitting in section 11.

Part A How many people in all are sitting in sections 10 and 11?

Answer ___________

Regroup when the sum of the digits in a place is 10 or greater.

Part B Explain how you found your answer.

____

____

____

____

Lesson 5

Adding Equal Groups

2.OA.3, 2.OA.4

Even numbers end in 0, 2, 4, 6, or 8.

2, 14, 26, 38, 40

Odd numbers end in 1, 3, 5, 7, or 9.

3, 15, 27, 39, 41

Every odd number is 1 more than an even number.

4 + 1 = 5
24 + 1 = 25

Every even number is 1 less than an odd number.

7 − 1 = 6
29 − 1 = 28

When you add a number to itself, the sum is always even.

2 + 2 = 4
5 + 5 = 10
11 + 11 = 22
30 + 30 = 60

You can count **even numbers** by 2's.

Is 14 even or odd?

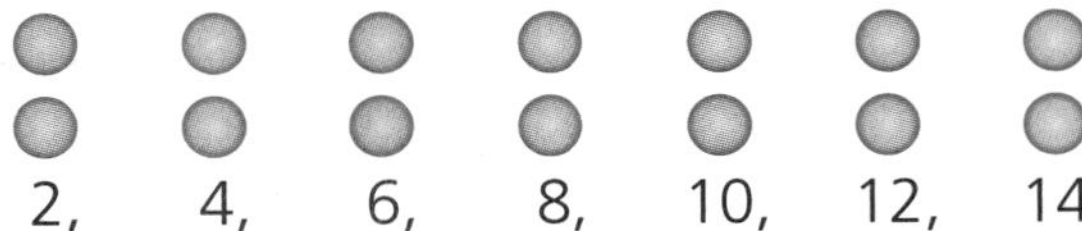

2, 4, 6, 8, 10, 12, 14

The number 14 is even.

You cannot count **odd numbers** by 2's. There is always one left.

Is 13 even or odd?

2, 4, 6, 8, 10, 12, + 1 = 13

The number 13 is odd.

You can add to find the total number in equal groups.

How many total squares are in this model?

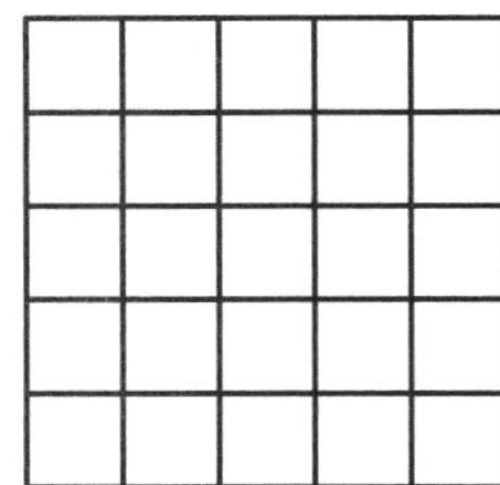

The model shows 5 rows of 5 squares.

Add to find the total number of squares:

5 + 5 + 5 + 5 + 5 = 25

You can also count by 5's: 5, 10, 15, 20, 25

Read each problem. Circle the letter of the best answer.

SAMPLE Which of these groups has an even number of circles?

A ●●●●● ●●●●●

C ●●●●● ●●●●

B ●●●● ●●●

D ●●● ●●

The correct answer is A. You can count even numbers by 2's. There is nothing left over. You cannot count odd numbers by 2's. There is always 1 left over. In choice A, you can count the group by 2's: 2, 4, 6, 8, 10. The other choices all have 1 left over. They show odd numbers.

1 Mrs. Woods stores decorations in the box below.

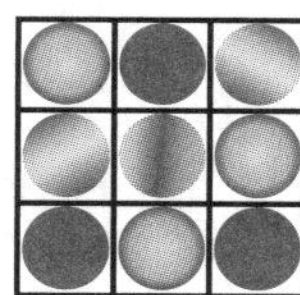

How many decorations are in the box in all?

A 3 **C** 6

B 5 **D** 9

2 Which number sentence can you use to find the total number of squares?

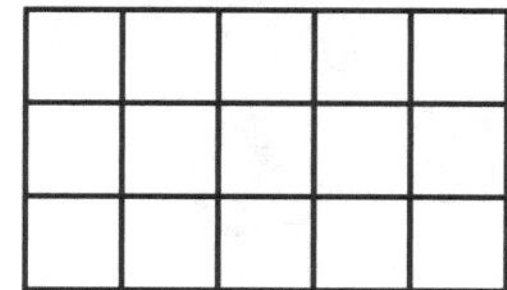

A 3 + 5 **C** 5 + 5 + 5

B 3 + 3 + 3 **D** 3 + 5 + 3 + 5

3 Which of these will have an even number as a sum?

A 6 + 7 **C** 7 + 8

B 7 + 7 **D** 8 + 9

4 Eric has this group of counters.

○ ○ ○ ○ ○ ○ ○ ○
○ ○ ○ ○ ○ ○ ○ ○

He adds 1 counter to the group. What is true about the number of counters after Eric adds 1 counter?

A The number is even.

B The number is odd.

C The number is not even or odd.

D The number is both even and odd.

Read each problem. Write your answer.

SAMPLE Look at the model below.

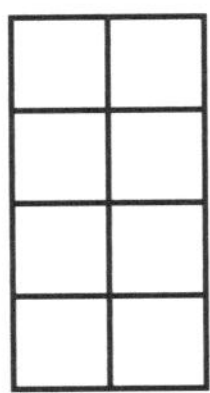

Write and solve a number sentence to find the total number of squares in this model.

Answer ______________________

The number sentence is 2 + 2 + 2 + 2 = 8 squares. You use repeated addition to find the total number of squares. This means you add the same number a certain number of times. There are 2 squares in each row. There are 4 rows. Add 2 four times. The sum is 8.

5 Look at the stars below.

Is the total number of circles even or odd?

Answer ______________

6 Zack has some round candies.
He put them in rows.

How many candies does Zack have in all?
Show your work.

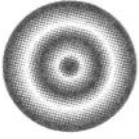  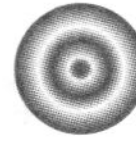

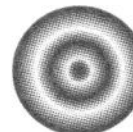  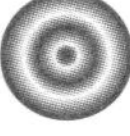

Answer ________

Read each problem. Write your answer to each part.

7 Mr. Groff put the students in his class into pairs.

Does every student have a partner?

Part A Explain how you can tell if the number of students is even or odd. Do not count the number of students.

____

____

Part B A new student comes to Mr. Groff's class. Is the total number of students now even or odd? Explain how you know.

____

____

8 Look at the model below.

Part A Write a number sentence to find the total number of squares. Find the total number of squares.

Answer ______________________

Part B Is the total number of squares odd or even?

Answer ______________

REVIEW

Addition

Read each problem. Circle the letter of the best answer.

1 What is the sum of 12 and 3?

A 14 **C** 16

B 15 **D** 17

2 Brandon had some oranges. He counted them by 2's. There was one orange left. What is true about the total number of oranges?

A It is odd.

B It is even.

C It is not even or odd.

D It is both even and odd.

3 There were 36 slices of cheese pizza. There were 42 slices of pepperoni pizza. How many slices of pizza were there in all?

A 68 **C** 78

B 70 **D** 80

4 Add:

$$\begin{array}{r} 760 \\ +\ 10 \\ \hline \end{array}$$

A 760 **C** 860

B 770 **D** 870

5 A snack stand sold 158 hot dogs. It sold 263 hamburgers. How many hot dogs and hamburgers did the stand sell in all?

A 311 **C** 411

B 321 **D** 421

6 Add:

$$\begin{array}{r} 62 \\ 14 \\ 29 \\ +11 \\ \hline \end{array}$$

A 106 **C** 116

B 107 **D** 117

Read each problem. Write your answer.

7 What is 100 more than 800?

Answer __________

8 Joey laid some playing cards on the table.

Is the total number of playing cards even or odd?

Answer ____________________

9 What doubles fact can you use to add 4 + 5?

Answer ____________________

10 A gardener planted 29 oak trees. He planted 45 pine trees. How many trees did he plant in all?

Answer __________

11 Write a number sentence to find the total number of squares in this model. Solve the number sentence.

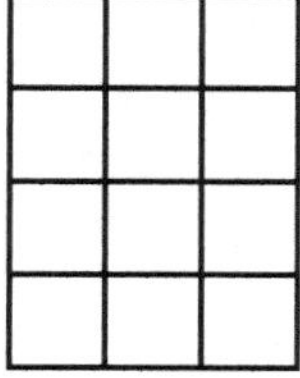

Answer ______________________________

Read each problem. Write your answer to each part.

12 The table below shows the weights of four dogs.

DOGS' WEIGHTS

Dog	Weight (in pounds)
Cooper	24
Buddy	13
Tank	36
Dane	28

Part A What is the total weight of these four dogs?

Answer ______________________________

Part B Explain how you found your answer.

____

____

____

13 On Monday, 427 people saw a play. On Tuesday, 371 people saw the play.

Part A How many people saw the play in all?

Answer __________

Part B Explain how you found your answer.

____

____

____

Unit 3

Subtraction

- **Lesson 1 Subtraction Basic Facts** reviews basic subtraction facts to 20.
- **Lesson 2 Subtracting 10 and 100** reviews subtracting 10 and 100 from two- and three-digit numbers.
- **Lesson 3 Subtracting Whole Numbers** reviews subtracting two- and three-digit numbers.
- **Lesson 4 Subtracting Whole Numbers with Regrouping** reviews subtracting two- and three-digit numbers when you have to regroup.

Lesson 1

Subtraction Basic Facts

2.OA.2

Subtract to compare numbers.

Subtract to find how many are left.

Subtract to find a missing part.

A **fact family** is four number sentences that use the same three numbers.

Fact families have two addition sentences and two subtraction sentences.

The answer to a subtraction problem is called the **difference.**

7 − 5 = 2 ← Difference

Subtract to find how many are left. It is important to know the basic subtraction facts. Basic facts will help you do harder subtraction.

You can use different strategies to subtract. Then you can do many subtraction problems in your head.

You can use fact families.

What is the difference of 8 − 6?

Think of the fact family that uses 8 and 6:

2 + 6 = 8	6 + 2 = 8
8 − 6 = 2	8 − 2 = 6

The difference is 2.

Fact families show you how three numbers relate to each other. This will help you know basic subtraction facts.

You can **decompose,** or break apart, a number.

Subtract: 15 − 8
Think of 8 as 5 and 3.
Subtract: 15 − 5 − 3
15 − 5 = 10, 10 − 3 = 7
So, 15 − 8 = 7.

Addition and subtraction are opposites. So you can use addition to check subtraction.

Check: 9 − 4 = 5

Add to check: 5 + 4 = 9
The subtraction is correct.

Read each problem. Circle the letter of the best answer.

SAMPLE Subtract:

$$12 - 8 = \square$$

A 4 **B** 5 **C** 6 **D** 7

The correct answer is A. Think of 8 as 2 and 6. Subtract 2 from 12: 12 − 2 = 10. Then subtract 6 from 10: 10 − 6 = 4. You can also think of the fact family that includes 12 and 8: 4 + 8 = 12, 8 + 4 = 12, 12 − 4 = 8, and 12 − 8 = 4.

1 Subtract:

$$9 - 3 = \square$$

A 4

B 5

C 6

D 7

2 What is the difference between 10 and 5?

A 6

B 5

C 4

D 3

3 What addition fact can you use to check 16 − 7 = 9?

A 6 + 10 = 16

B 7 + 11 = 18

C 6 + 9 = 15

D 7 + 9 = 16

4 Amber had 8 pieces of gum. She gave 5 pieces away. How many pieces of gum did Amber have left?

A 2

B 3

C 4

D 5

5 Heath wants to subtract 14 − 9. What is the best way to decompose 9 to solve this problem?

A 4 and 5

B 3 and 6

C 2 and 7

D 1 and 8

6 Subtract:

$$18 - 9 = \square$$

A 7

B 8

C 9

D 10

Read each problem. Write your answer.

SAMPLE What number sentences are missing from this fact family?

$5 + 6 = 11$ $\qquad$ $6 + 5 = 11$

☐ $\qquad$ ☐

One of the missing number sentences is $11 - 6 = 5$. The other missing number sentence is $11 - 5 = 6$. A fact family uses the same three numbers. There are two addition facts. There are two subtraction facts.

7 Subtract:

$$7 - 3 = \square$$

Answer ____________

8 A picnic basket contained 6 sandwiches. Troy, Ben, and Marcus each ate a sandwich. How many sandwiches were left?

Answer ____________

9 Jamal wrote this fact family.

$4 + 6 = 10$ $\qquad$ $6 + 4 = 10$

$10 - 6 = 4$ $\qquad$ ☐

What number sentence is missing from this fact family?

Answer ________________________

Read each problem. Write your answer to each part.

10 Emma cut 13 stars out of paper. There were 8 yellow stars. The rest of the stars were orange.

How can you break apart 8 to make it easier to subtract?

Part A How many stars were orange?

Answer ___________

Part B Explain how you found your answer.

____

____

____

____

11 Rob wants to find the difference between 14 and 6.

Part A What is the difference between 14 and 6?

Answer ___________

Part B What addition problem can you use to check your answer? Explain why.

____

____

____

____

Lesson 2

Subtracting 10 and 100

2.NBT.8

The value of a digit depends on its place in a number.

Hundreds	Tens	Ones
4	9	5

To subtract tens, subtract the number of tens. Keep the number of ones the same.

75 − 10 = 65

To subtract hundreds, subtract the number of hundreds. Keep the ones and the tens the same.

751 − 100 = 651

You can use basic subtraction facts to help you subtract ten.

Subtract: 80 − 10
Think of 80 as 8 tens. Think of 10 as 1 ten.
8 tens − 1 ten = 7 tens
So, 80 − 10 = 70.

It is easy to subtract tens in your head. Just subtract the number of tens in each number. The ones digit stays the same.

Subtract: 86 − 10
There are 8 tens in 86. Think of 10 as 1 ten.
Subtract: 8 tens − 1 ten = 7 tens
There are still 6 ones.
So, 86 − 10 = 76.

You can use basic subtraction facts to help you subtract 100.

Subtract: 800 − 200
Think of 800 as 8 hundreds. Think of 200 as 2 hundreds.
8 hundreds − 2 hundreds = 6 hundreds
So, 800 − 200 = 600.

It is easy to subtract hundreds in your head. Just subtract the number of hundreds in each number. The tens and ones stay the same.

Subtract: 862 − 200
There are 8 hundreds in 862. Think of 200 as 2 hundreds.
Subtract: 8 hundreds − 2 hundreds = 6 hundreds
There are still 6 tens and 2 ones.
So, 862 − 200 = 662.

Read each problem. Circle the letter of the best answer.

SAMPLE Subtract:

$$45 - 20 = \square$$

A 15 **B** 20 **C** 25 **D** 30

The correct answer is C. Think of 20 as 2 tens. Think of 45 as 4 tens and 5 ones. Subtract the tens: 4 tens − 2 tens = 2 tens. The ones stay the same. So 45 − 20 = 25.

1 What basic fact can you use to subtract 70 − 30?

A 7 − 3 = 4

B 7 − 4 = 3

C 7 − 2 = 5

D 7 − 6 = 1

2 Subtract:

$$900 - 700 = \square$$

A 500

B 400

C 300

D 200

3 Nina used the basic fact 6 − 3 = 3 to solve a subtraction problem. Which subtraction problem could Nina have solved?

A $600 - 30 = \square$

B $600 - 300 = \square$

C $60 - 300 = \square$

D $630 - 30 = \square$

4 Subtract:

$$58 - 20 = \square$$

A 20

B 28

C 30

D 38

5 Xun has 4 packs with 10 crackers in each pack. He eats 1 pack of 10 crackers. How many crackers are left?

A 40

B 39

C 30

D 3

6 Find the difference.

$$724 - 600 = \square$$

A 100

B 124

C 200

D 224

Read each problem. Write your answer.

SAMPLE Greg wants to solve this problem.

$$90 - 60 = \square$$

What basic subtraction fact can Greg use to solve this problem?

Answer ____________________

Greg can use this basic subtraction fact: 9 − 6 = 3. Think of 90 as 9 tens. Think of 60 as 6 tens. Subtract: 9 tens − 6 tens = 3 tens. You can use the basic fact 9 − 6 = 3. The ones digit stays 0.

7 A store has 300 T-shirts. One week, the store sold 100 T-shirts. How many T-shirts were left?

Answer __________

8 Explain how you can use a basic subtraction fact to help you solve 526 − 200.

____

____

____

9 Find the difference.

$$84 - 40 = \square$$

Answer __________

Read each problem. Write your answer to each part.

10 Chase has 478 building blocks. He uses 200 blocks to build a tower.

How many hundreds are in 478?

Part A How many building blocks are left?

Answer ___________

Part B Explain how you found your answer.

____

____

____

11 Rita wants to read 25 pages this evening. So far, she has read 10 pages.

Part A How many more pages must Rita read?

Answer ___________

Part B What basic fact did you use to help you find your answer? Explain.

____

____

____

LESSON 3

Subtracting Whole Numbers

2.NBT.5, 2.NBT.7, 2.NBT.9

The answer in a subtraction problem is called the difference.

7 − 4 = 3 ← Difference

Always subtract from right to left.

Hundreds Ones
↓ ↓
567
↑
Tens

Addition and subtraction are opposites. You can add to check subtraction.

25 − 10 = 15
because
15 + 10 = 25

You subtract numbers for different reasons. You can subtract to compare numbers. You can subtract to find how many are left. You can subtract to find a missing part.

Models can help you subtract.

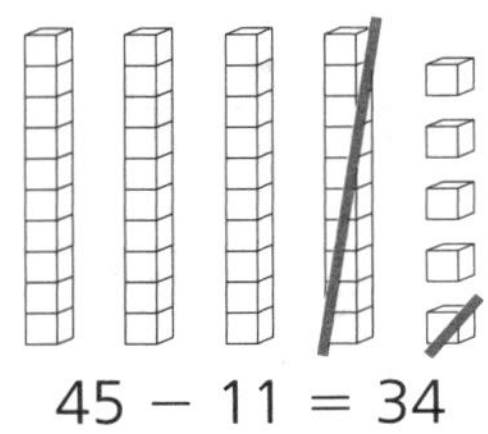

45 − 11 = 34

Subtract numbers by subtracting the digits in the same places.

Subtract: 56 − 12

Subtract the ones.	Subtract the tens.
56 −12 4	56 −12 44

So, 56 − 12 is 44.

Subtract: 758 − 327

Subtract the ones.	Subtract the tens.	Subtract the hundreds.
758 −327 1	758 −327 31	758 −327 431

So, 758 − 327 is 431.

Read each problem. Circle the letter of the best answer.

SAMPLE A box contained 62 light bulbs. Chad dropped the box. Thirty-one light bulbs broke. How many light bulbs did ***not*** break?

A 20 **B** 21 **C** 30 **D** 31

The correct answer is D. Subtract the number of broken light bulbs from the total number of light bulbs. First subtract the ones. Then subtract the tens: 62 − 31 = 31.

1 Subtract:

$$\begin{array}{r} 387 \\ -216 \\ \hline \end{array}$$

A 170

B 171

C 180

D 181

2 Pam did this subtraction problem.

94 − 52 = 42

Which addition problem shows that Pam is correct?

A 40 + 50 = 90

B 94 + 42 = 136

C 42 + 52 = 94

D 94 + 52 = 146

3 There are 46 second graders who play softball. There are 35 second graders who play soccer. How many more second graders play softball than play soccer?

A 11 **C** 21

B 12 **D** 81

4 Ryan has 859 pictures on his camera. He deletes 149 pictures. How many pictures are left?

A 600 **C** 700

B 610 **D** 710

5 Find the difference.

78 − 33 = □

A 35 **C** 45

B 36 **D** 46

Read each problem. Write your answer.

SAMPLE Li did this subtraction problem.

$$648 - 543 = 105$$

What addition problem can Li do to check his answer?

Answer ______________________________

Li can add 105 + 543. If his sum is 648, his work is correct. Subtraction is the opposite of addition. You can add the difference and the number that was subtracted. The sum should be the first number.

6 Alexis has the base ten blocks shown below.

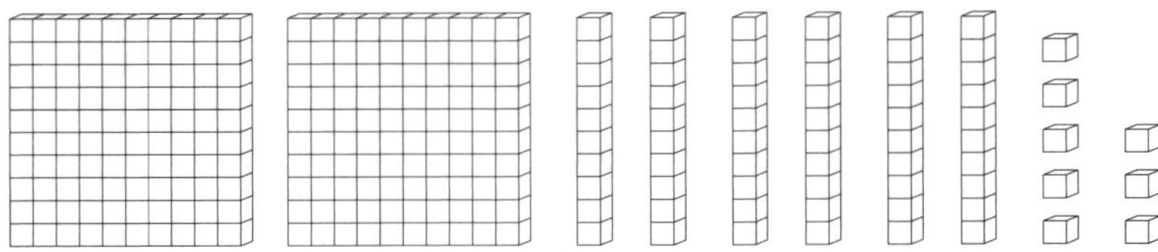

Alexis wants to subtract 268 − 124. Explain how Alexis can use these blocks to help her.

____

____

____

____

7 There were 78 pretzels in a jar. Students ate 62 of them. How many pretzels are left?

Answer __________

Read each problem. Write your answer to each part.

8 Hamish is making signs for the school play. He made 24 big signs. He made 56 small signs.

Hamish made more small signs than big signs. Which number do you subtract?

Part A How many more small signs than big signs did Hamish make?

Answer ____________

Part B What addition problem can you use to check your answer? Explain why.

____

____

____

____

9 Binta wants to do this subtraction problem.

$$936 - 314 = \square$$

Part A Explain how Binta could use base ten blocks to help her do this problem.

____

____

____

____

Part B What is the answer to the subtraction problem?

Answer ____________

Lesson 4

Subtracting Whole Numbers with Regrouping

2.NBT.5, 2.NBT.7, 2.NBT.9

The difference is the answer to a subtraction problem.

4 − 2 = 2
↑
Difference

Regroup 1 ten as 10 ones.

Regroup 1 hundred as 10 tens.

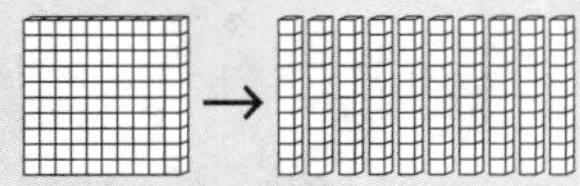

Addition and subtraction are opposites. You can add to check subtraction.

425 − 114 = 311
because
311 + 114 = 425

Sometimes a digit is not large enough to subtract from. Then you need to regroup the next place to the left.

Subtract the digits in the same places. Subtract from right to left.

Find the difference of 437 and 289.

```
  2 17
 4 3 7
−2 8 9
     8
```

Subtract the ones. You cannot subtract 9 ones from 7 ones. Regroup 3 tens as 2 tens and 10 ones. Combine 10 ones and 7 ones for 17 ones. Subtract: 17 − 9 = 8

```
   12
 3 2 17
 4 3 7
−2 8 9
   4 8
```

Subtract the tens. You cannot subtract 8 tens from 2 tens. Regroup 4 hundreds as 3 hundreds and 10 tens. Combine 10 tens and 2 tens for 12 tens. Subtract: 12 − 8 = 4

```
   12
 3 2 17
 4 3 7
−2 8 9
 1 4 8
```

Subtract the hundreds: 3 − 2 = 1

The difference is 148.

Read each problem. Circle the letter of the best answer.

SAMPLE Subtract:

$$73 - 46 = \square$$

A 24 **B** 27 **C** 33 **D** 34

The correct answer is B. Subtract the ones. Then subtract the tens. You cannot subtract 6 ones from 3 ones. So regroup 1 ten as 10 ones. Combine the ones for 13 ones. Then subtract: 13 ones − 6 ones = 7 ones. Subtract the tens: 6 tens − 4 tens = 2 tens. The difference is 27.

1 There were 974 people at a hockey game. The first 425 people won a free hat. How many people did ***not*** win a free hat?

A 559

B 551

C 549

D 545

2 Yoshi picked 30 flowers. There were 17 roses. The rest were daisies. How many flowers were daisies?

A 13

B 17

C 23

D 27

3 Subtract:

$$\begin{array}{r} 619 \\ -378 \\ \hline \end{array}$$

A 239

B 241

C 341

D 361

4 A clown was carrying 41 balloons. There were 23 red balloons. The rest were yellow. How many yellow balloons were there?

A 28 **C** 18

B 22 **D** 12

5 Find the difference.

$$564 - 487 = \square$$

A 77 **C** 123

B 87 **D** 187

Read each problem. Write your answer.

SAMPLE Devon collects postcards. She has 352 postcards in all. She has 179 postcards from other countries. The rest are from the United States. How many postcards are from the United States?

Answer ___________

There are 173 postcards that are from the United States. To find the answer, subtract 352 − 179. You will need to regroup twice:

$$\begin{array}{r} \scriptstyle 14 \\ \scriptstyle 2\not{4}12 \\ \not{3}\not{5}\not{2} \\ -179 \\ \hline 173 \end{array}$$

6 There are 61 cars in a parking lot. There are 27 black cars. How many cars are other colors? Show your work.

Answer ___________

7 One weekend, 728 people saw a certain movie. There were 564 people who liked the movie. The rest did not like the movie. How many people did ***not*** like the movie?

Answer ___________

8 Subtract:

$$\begin{array}{r} 93 \\ -34 \\ \hline \end{array}$$

Answer ___________

Read each problem. Write your answer to each part.

9 Shelby received $45 for her birthday. She bought a shirt that cost $18.

Part A How much money did Shelby have left?

Answer ____________

Part B Explain how you found your answer.

____

____

____

10 A train has 950 seats for passengers. One day, there were 742 people on the train.

Part A How many seats were empty on the train?

Always regroup one place to the left.

Answer ____________

Part B Explain how you found your answer.

____

____

____

REVIEW

Subtraction

Read each problem. Circle the letter of the best answer.

1 Subtract:

$$\begin{array}{r} 15 \\ -\ 7 \\ \hline \end{array}$$

A 6

B 7

C 8

D 9

2 Noel got 28 e-mails. She deleted 17 e-mails. How many e-mails did Noel keep?

A 18

B 17

C 12

D 11

3 What is 10 less than 75?

A 55

B 65

C 70

D 80

4 Quincy lives 273 miles from his grandmother. He is going to visit. He has traveled 128 miles so far. How many more miles does Quincy have to travel?

A 142

B 145

C 150

D 155

5 What addition fact can you use to check $17 - 9 = 8$?

A $8 + 9 = 17$

B $17 + 9 = 26$

C $8 + 8 = 16$

D $9 + 9 = 18$

6 Subtract:

$$536 - 300 = \square$$

A 200

B 236

C 300

D 336

Read each problem. Write your answer.

7 There are 763 students at Lincoln Elementary School. There are 486 girls. How many boys are there?

Answer ___________

8 Explain how you can use a basic subtraction fact to help you solve 98 − 30.

____

____

____

9 Find the difference.

$$\begin{array}{r} 62 \\ -47 \\ \hline \end{array}$$

Answer ___________

10 Look at this fact family.

3 + 9 = 12	9 + 3 = 12
12 − 3 = 9	?

What number sentence is missing from this fact family?

Answer ______________________

Read each problem. Write your answer to each part.

11 There were 450 geese on a lake. Then 340 geese flew away.

Part A How many geese were still on the lake?

Answer ___________

Part B Explain how you found your answer.

____

____

____

____

12 Sam wanted to kick a ball 41 feet. He kicked it only 28 feet.

Part A How many feet farther did the ball need to go?

Answer ___________

Part B Explain how you found your answer.

____

____

____

____

Using Addition and Subtraction

- **Lesson 1 Addition Number Sentences** reviews how to write and solve an addition number sentence.
- **Lesson 2 Subtraction Number Sentences** reviews how to write and solve a subtraction number sentence.
- **Lesson 3 Word Problems** reviews how to solve word problems using pictures and number sentences.

LESSON 1

Addition Number Sentences

2.OA.1

Things that are **equal** have the same value.

An **equation** is a number sentence that uses an equals sign. The two sides of an equation always balance. This means that they have the same value.

You can think of fact families to help you find a missing number. A fact family is four number sentences that use the same three numbers.

$4 + 3 = 7$
$3 + 4 = 7$
$7 - 3 = 4$
$7 - 4 = 3$

A **number sentence** shows something about numbers. It uses numbers and symbols.

The symbol + means "plus." It shows addition.

The symbol = means "is equal to."

What does the number sentence below say?

$$4 + 3 = 7$$

Read the numbers and symbols. This number sentence says, "4 plus 3 is equal to 7."

Sometimes a number is missing in a number sentence. A box or another shape stands for the missing number.

$$4 + \square = 7$$

This number sentence says, "4 plus some number is equal to 7."

How can you find the missing number?

Remember that addition and subtraction are opposites.

Subtract: $7 - 4 = 3$. So $4 + 3 = 7$.
The missing number is 3.

You can also think of the basic addition fact.

Think: "4 plus what number is equal to 7?"

You know the basic addition fact $4 + 3 = 7$.
The missing number is 3.

Read each problem. Circle the letter of the best answer.

SAMPLE What is the missing number in this number sentence?

$$7 + \bigcirc = 16$$

A 8 B 9 C 16 D 24

The correct answer is B. The circle stands for the missing number. Addition and subtraction are opposites. You can subtract to find the missing number: 16 − 7 = 9. So the missing number is 9. Remember to check your answer. Put your answer in place of the circle. Then add: 7 + 9 = 16.

1 Which number sentence means "some number plus 5 equals 28"?

A $\square + 28 = 5$

B $28 + 5 = \square$

C $\square + 5 = 28$

D $28 + 5 + \square$

2 What number is missing in this number sentence?

$$12 + \square = 18$$

A 6 C 12

B 7 D 18

3 Which number sentence is balanced?

A $5 + 6 = 12$

B $9 + 4 = 14$

C $3 + 8 = 10$

D $4 + 7 = 11$

4 Find the missing number in this number sentence.

$$\bigcirc + 25 = 75$$

A 40

B 50

C 80

D 100

5 Jenny wrote a number sentence. It means "20 plus some number equals 32." Which of these is Jenny's number sentence?

A $20 + \bigcirc = 32$

B $20 + 32 = \bigcirc$

C $32 + \bigcirc = 20$

D $32 + 20 = \bigcirc$

Read each problem. Write your answer.

SAMPLE Write a number sentence that means "10 plus some number equals 43." Use a □ for the missing number.

Answer ____________________

The number sentence is 10 + □ = 43. The + symbol means "plus." The = symbol means "is equal to." The □ stands for "some number." So the number sentence is 10 + □ = 43.

6 Ashton wants to find the missing number in this number sentence.

$$\square + 7 = 13$$

He says the missing number is 4. Is Ashton correct? Explain.

____

____

7 What number is missing in this number sentence?

$$22 + \bigcirc = 30$$

Answer __________

8 Write a number sentence that means "14 plus some number equals 18." Use a □ for the missing number.

Answer ____________________

Read the problem. Write your answer to each part.

9 Mr. Costa wrote a number sentence on the board. It said, "A number plus 15 equals 45."

Part A Write Mr. Costa's number sentence. Use a ○ for the missing number.

Answer ______________________________

Part B What is the missing number in this number sentence? Explain how you found your answer.

What operation is the opposite of addition?

____

____

____

____

____

Lesson 2

Subtraction Number Sentences

2.OA.1

Two things that are equal have the same value.

An equation is a number sentence that uses an equals sign. The two sides of an equation always balance. This means they have the same value.

Addition and subtraction are opposites. You can add to check subtraction.

$9 - 4 = 5$
because
$5 + 4 = 9$

A number sentence shows something about numbers. It uses numbers and symbols.

The symbol − means "minus." It shows subtraction. The symbol = means "is equal to."

What does the number sentence below say?

$$9 - 5 = 4$$

Read the numbers and symbols. This number sentence says, "9 minus 5 is equal to 4."

Sometimes a number is missing in a number sentence. A box or another shape stands for the missing number.

$$9 - \square = 4$$

This number sentence says, "9 minus some number is equal to 4."

How can you find the missing number?

You know the difference is 4. You can subtract the difference from 9 to find the missing number.
Subtract: $9 - 4 = 5$
The missing number is 5.
So, $9 - 5 = 4$.

A fact family can also help you find the missing number.

$4 + \square = 9$ $\qquad$ $\square + 4 = 9$
$9 - \square = 4$ $\qquad$ $9 - 4 = \square$

This fact family uses 4, □, and 9. Look at all the number sentences. The missing number is always 5.

Read each problem. Circle the letter of the best answer.

SAMPLE What number is missing from this number sentence?

$\square - 7 = 11$

A 17 **B** 18 **C** 19 **D** 20

The correct answer is B. This number sentence says, "A number minus 7 equals 11." Addition and subtraction are opposite operations. Add to find the missing number: 11 + 7 = 18. Remember to check your answer. Put your answer in the place of the box. See if the equation is balanced: 18 − 7 = 11.

1 Look at this number sentence.

$28 - \square = 24$

How should you read this number sentence?

A 28 minus some number equals 24.

B 28 minus 24 equals some number.

C 24 plus some number equals 28.

D 24 minus some number equals 28.

2 What is the missing number in this number sentence?

$16 - \square = 6$

A 6

B 8

C 9

D 10

3 Which number sentence means "some number minus 8 equals 40"?

A $8 - \bigcirc = 40$

B $40 - \bigcirc = 8$

C $\bigcirc - 8 = 40$

D $\bigcirc - 40 = 8$

4 What number is missing in this number sentence?

$\bigcirc - 5 = 15$

A 10 **C** 25

B 20 **D** 30

5 Which number sentence is ***not*** balanced?

A 12 − 8 = 4 **C** 14 − 5 = 9

B 13 − 6 = 7 **D** 15 − 9 = 4

Read each problem. Write your answer.

SAMPLE Write a number sentence that means "some number minus 10 equals 22." Use a ○ for the missing number.

Answer ____________________

The number sentence is ○ − 10 = 22. The ○ stands for the missing number. The − sign means "minus." The = sign means "is equal to."

6 What number is missing in this number sentence?

35 − □ = 31

Answer __________

7 Vicki found the missing number in this number sentence.

17 − ○ = 9

She says the missing number is 8. Is Vicki correct? Explain how you know.

____

____

8 Write a number sentence that means "36 minus some number equals 20." Use a □ for the missing number.

Answer ______________________________

Read the problem. Write your answer to each part.

9 Will wrote a number sentence. It said, "Some number minus 3 is 10."

Part A Write Will's number sentence. Use a ○ for the missing number.

Answer ______________________

Part B What is the missing number in this number sentence? Explain how you found your answer.

What operation is the opposite of subtraction?

____

____

____

____

____

Lesson 3

Word Problems

2.OA.1

Take these steps to solve a word problem.

1. **Read** the problem.
2. **Think** about the problem.
   What do I know?
   What must I find out?
   How can I find the answer?
3. **Solve** the problem.
4. **Check** your answer. Does it make sense?

When you use a picture, you do not have to draw the actual object. You can use tally marks (𝍸). Or you can use dots (•). You can use any other symbol that is easy for you.

Use a shape to show the missing number in a number sentence. You can use any shape.

□ ○ △

Word problems tell number stories.

You can draw a picture to help you solve a word problem.

Lucy had 4 dollars. She got 6 more dollars. How many dollars does she have in all?

Think: You know how much Lucy has. You know how much she gets. You need to find how much she has in all. So you need to add.

Draw a picture.

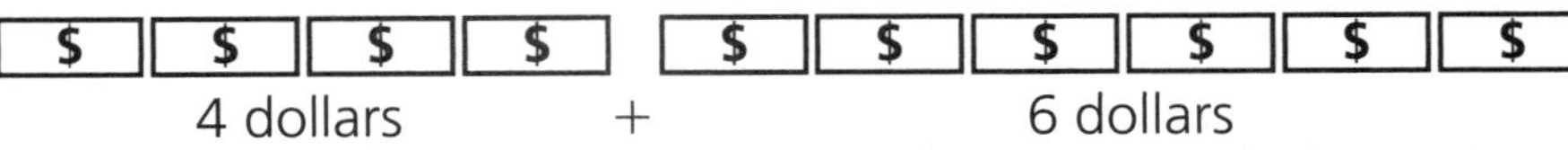

4 dollars + 6 dollars

Count the total number of dollars: 10
Lucy has 10 dollars in all.

You can write a number sentence to solve a word problem.

Vic had some jelly beans. He ate 7 jelly beans. Then he had 5 jelly beans left. How many jelly beans did Vic have to start?

Think: You know how many jelly beans Vic ate. You know how many he has left. You need to find how many he had to start. Use subtraction.

Write a subtraction sentence. Use a □ for the missing number.

$$\square - 7 = 5$$

Solve the number sentence: $5 + 7 = 12$, so $\square = 12$

Check your answer: $12 - 7 = 5$

Vic had 12 jelly beans to start.

Read each problem. Circle the letter of the best answer.

SAMPLE Laila picked 5 flowers. Then she picked 6 more flowers. Laila gave 4 of her flowers to her mom. How many flowers does Laila have left?

A 11 **B** 10 **C** 7 **D** 6

The correct answer is C. This word problem takes two steps to solve. First find how many flowers Laila picked in all. Add. You can draw a picture: ✿✿✿✿✿ + ✿✿✿✿✿✿. There are 11 flowers in all. Then Laila gave some away. Subtract. Use your picture: ✿✿✿✿✿✿✿✿✿✿✿ (4 crossed out). There are 7 flowers left.

1 There are 25 children at the ice rink. There are 8 children sitting on the benches. The rest are skating. How many children are skating?

A 17 **C** 15

B 16 **D** 14

2 Asako drew a picture to solve this word problem.

> Seth ate 3 cookies. Eva ate 8 cookies. How many cookies did they eat in all?

Which picture could Asako use to solve this word problem?

A ○○○○○ØØØ

B ○○○ØØØØØØØØ

C ○○○ + ○○○○○○○○

D ○○○○○○○○○○○ + ○○○

3 A box contains 48 crayons and markers. There are 27 crayons. Which number sentence can you use to find the number of markers?

A 48 + □ = 27

B 48 + 27 = □

C 27 − □ = 48

D 48 − □ = 27

4 There are 25 students in Mr. Suarez's class. There are 23 students in Ms. Valley's class. One day, 4 students were not in school. How many students were there in all?

A 48 **C** 24

B 44 **D** 21

Read each problem. Write your answer.

SAMPLE Emily wants to collect 30 charms for her bracelet. She has 14 charms so far. How many more charms does Emily need?

Answer ____________

Emily needs 16 more charms. Write a number sentence to find the answer. You know how many charms Emily wants. You know how many she has. Add to find a total. Use a ○ for the missing number: 14 + ○ = 30. Find the missing number by subtracting: 30 − 14 = 16. Check your answer: 14 + 16 = 30. The answer 16 is correct.

5 Tom has 65 baseball cards. He buys some more cards. Now he has 79 cards. How many baseball cards did Tom buy? Show your work.

Answer ____________

6 There were 48 children at the playground. There were 24 children playing on the jungle gym. The rest of the children were playing on the ball field. Write a number sentence you can use to find the number of children playing on the ball field.

Answer ____________________________________

7 Mrs. Murphy made 12 sandwiches. Her children ate 5 sandwiches. How many sandwiches were left? Draw a picture here to help you find the answer.

Answer ____________

Read the problem. Write your answer to each part.

8 Carlos collected 68 leaves. Then he collected 13 more leaves. Finally he threw away 24 of the leaves.

Part A How many leaves does Carlos have in all? Show your work.

Is it easier to draw a picture or write a number sentence for this problem?

Answer __________

Part B Explain how you found your answer.

____

____

____

____

REVIEW

Using Addition and Subtraction

Read each problem. Circle the letter of the best answer.

1 Which number sentence means "24 plus some number equals 60"?

A 24 + 60 = ☐

B 24 + ☐ = 60

C 60 + ☐ = 24

D 60 + 24 = ☐

2 What is the missing number in this number sentence?

25 − ◯ = 10

A 5 **C** 15

B 10 **D** 20

3 There were 14 students in line for lunch. There were 8 students sitting at the lunch table. Which picture could you use to find how many students there were in all?

A ●●●●●●øøøøøøøø

B ●●●●●●●●●●●●●● + ●●●●●●●●

C øøøøøøøø

D ●●●●●●●●●●●●●● + ●●●●

4 What number is missing in this number sentence?

☐ + 11 = 32

A 21 **C** 33

B 22 **D** 43

5 Look at this number sentence.

◯ − 7 = 23

What does this number sentence mean?

A 7 minus some number equals 23.

B 7 plus 23 equals some number.

C Some number minus 23 equals 7.

D Some number minus 7 equals 23.

6 Grace had 8 rings. There were 3 gold rings. The rest of the rings were silver. How many silver rings did Grace have?

A 11 **C** 6

B 10 **D** 5

Read each problem. Write your answer.

7 Write a number sentence that means "some number plus 10 equals 43." Use a □ for the missing number.

Answer ______________________________

8 Kevin found the missing number in this number sentence.

$$\bigcirc - 6 = 24$$

Kevin says the missing number is 18. Is Kevin correct? Explain.

____

____

____

____

9 Justin is playing a card game. He has 9 cards in his hand. He pulls some more cards. Then he lays down 3 cards. He has 12 cards left in his hand. How many cards did Justin pull? Show your work.

Answer __________

Read each problem. Write your answer to each part.

10 A number sentence means "27 minus some number equals 18."

Part A Write the number sentence with numbers and symbols. Use a □ for the missing number.

Answer ______________________________

Part B What is the missing number in the number sentence? Explain how you found your answer.

____

____

____

____

11 Ms. Nguyen cut a cake into 32 pieces. Some of the pieces were eaten. There were 12 pieces of cake left.

Part A How many pieces of cake were eaten? Draw a picture to help you find the answer.

Answer __________

Part B Explain how you found your answer.

____

____

____

____

UNIT 5

Measurement

- **Lesson 1 Customary Units of Length** reviews how to estimate lengths with inches and feet.
- **Lesson 2 Metric Units of Length** reviews how to estimate lengths with centimeters and meters.
- **Lesson 3 Measuring Lengths** reviews how to use an inch ruler and a centimeter ruler to measure lengths.
- **Lesson 4 Adding and Subtracting Lengths** reviews how to solve problems by adding and subtracting lengths.
- **Lesson 5 Time** reviews how to tell time on an analog clock and a digital clock.
- **Lesson 6 Money** reviews how to solve problems by counting bills and coins.

Lesson 1

Customary Units of Length

2.MD.3

An inch is a **standard unit.** A foot is also a standard unit. A standard unit is always the same.

You can measure length with a **non-standard unit.** A non-standard unit is ***not*** always the same length.

Non-standard units:
- paper clip
- pencil
- finger
- coin

Width is how wide something is.

Height is how tall something is.

A **ruler** is a measurement tool. You use it to measure length, width, or height. Many rulers are marked in inches.

When you estimate, you make a good guess. You use what you already know to make your guess.

Length is how long something is. You also use length to find how wide or how tall something is.

In the United States, we use the **customary system** to measure. We use inches and feet to measure length.

An **inch** is a small unit of measurement. It is about the length of a quarter.

A **foot** is larger than an inch. There are 12 inches in 1 foot.

You **measure** something to find its size. You can use tools to measure. Sometimes you do not have a tool. You must **estimate** the length of something.

What is the length of this pencil?

You know that a quarter is about an inch. Think: About how many quarters long is the pencil?

You could line up about 4 quarters along the pencil. The pencil is about 4 inches long. This is a good estimate.

Read each problem. Circle the letter of the best answer.

SAMPLE Heidi has this piece of yarn.

About how long is this piece of yarn?

A 3 inches **B** 6 inches **C** 3 feet **D** 6 feet

The correct answer is B. An inch is a small unit of length. Think about the length of a quarter. Imagine lining quarters up along the piece of yarn. You could fit about 6 quarters along the yarn. So the piece of yarn is about 6 inches long.

1 Pedro wants to measure the height of his bedroom door. He does not have a tool to use. What is a good estimate of the height of the door?

A 1 inch
B 1 foot
C 7 inches
D 7 feet

2 Tyrell is in second grade. He estimates that he is about 6 feet tall. Is this a good estimate?

A Yes, he is probably about 6 feet tall.

B No, he is probably about 6 inches tall.

C No, he is probably about 4 feet tall.

D No, he is probably about 4 inches tall.

3 Wendy uses this crayon to color.

About how long is Wendy's crayon?

A 1 inch
B 2 inches
C 3 inches
D 4 inches

4 Isabella has a student ID.

About how wide is Isabella's card?

A 1 inch
B 2 inches
C 1 foot
D 2 feet

Read each problem. Write your answer.

SAMPLE Meg wants to estimate the length of her favorite book. Which unit would be best to use—inches or feet?

Answer ____________________

> The best unit is inches. Think about a book you have held. Think about its length. A book is not a long object. Use a smaller unit to measure shorter objects. Inches are a small unit of length. Meg should measure her book using inches.

5 Estimate the length of your desk.

Answer ____________________

6 Estimate the height of your chair.

Answer ____________________

7 Luca wants to estimate the length of his dad's car. Which unit should Luca use—inches or feet? Explain how he will make the estimate.

____

____

____

____

Read the problem. Write your answer to each part.

8 Tanya used this paintbrush to paint a picture.

Think of an object that is about 1 inch long.

Part A About how long is the paintbrush?

Answer ____________________

Part B Explain how you made your estimate.

____

____

____

____

LESSON 2

Metric Units of Length

2.MD.3

A centimeter is a standard unit. A meter is also a standard unit. A standard unit is always the same.

You can measure length with a non-standard unit. A non-standard unit is ***not*** always the same length.

Non-standard units:
- paper clip
- pencil
- finger
- coin

A ruler is a measurement tool. You use it to measure length, width, or height. Rulers can be marked in centimeters.

When you estimate, you make a good guess. You use what you already know to make your guess.

Length is how long something is. You also use length to find how wide or how tall something is.

Many countries use the **metric system** to measure. This system uses centimeters and meters to measure length.

A **centimeter** is a small unit of measurement. It is about the width of a finger.

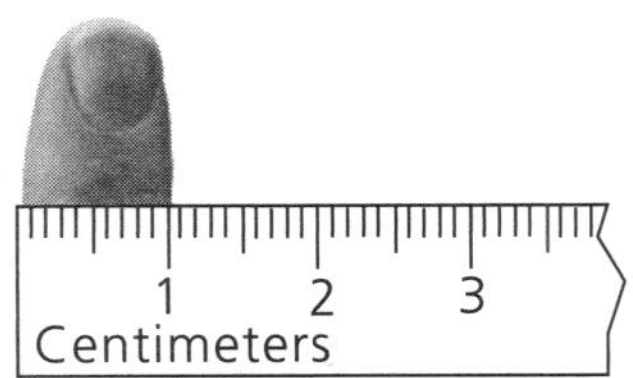

A **meter** is longer than a centimeter. There are 100 centimeters in 1 meter. A meter is about the length of a baseball bat.

Tools help you measure. Sometimes you do not have a tool. You must estimate the length of something.

What is the length of this pretzel stick?

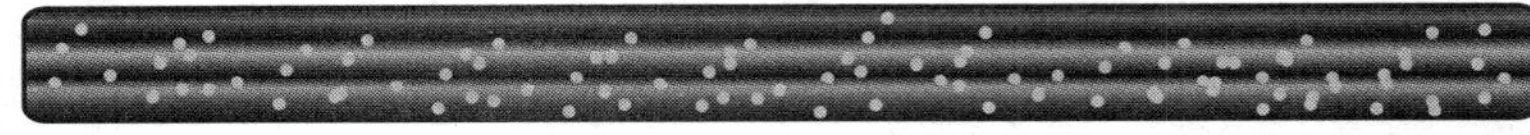

You know that your finger is about 1 centimeter wide. Measure the length of the pretzel stick with the width of your finger.

You can fit about 10 of your fingers along the pretzel stick. The pretzel stick is about 10 centimeters long. This is a good estimate.

Read each problem. Circle the letter of the best answer.

SAMPLE About how long is this pen?

A 3 centimeters

B 12 centimeters

C 3 meters

D 12 meters

The correct answer is B. A centimeter is a short unit. A meter is a long unit. The pen is too short to be 3 or 12 meters long. The width of your finger is about 1 centimeter. Think: How many finger widths are equal to the length of the pen? A good estimate is 12 centimeters.

1 Brett wants to estimate the height of his swing set. What is a good estimate for the height of a swing set?

A 3 centimeters

B 30 centimeters

C 3 meters

D 30 meters

2 Autumn measured the length of this nail.

About how long is this nail?

A 1 centimeter

B 8 centimeters

C 1 meter

D 8 meters

3 Which piece of string is about 5 centimeters long?

A 

B 

C 

D

4 Kadir is in second grade. He estimated that his sneaker is about 20 centimeters long. Is this a good estimate?

A Yes, it is probably about 20 centimeters long.

B No, it is probably about 2 centimeters long.

C No, it is probably about 20 meters long.

D No, it is probably about 2 meters long.

Read each problem. Write your answer.

SAMPLE Sydney wants to estimate the length of her necklace. Which unit would be best to use—centimeters or meters?

Answer ______________________

The best unit is centimeters. A necklace is worn around a person's neck. It is probably not longer than a meter. Centimeters are the best units to use to estimate its length.

5 Estimate the height from the floor to your desktop.

Answer ______________

6 Estimate the length of your classroom.

Answer ______________

7 Rico wants to estimate the height of a tree in his backyard. Which unit would be best to use—centimeters or meters? Explain how he will make the estimate.

____

____

____

____

Read the problem. Write your answer to each part.

8 Mr. Harper has this stapler on his desk.

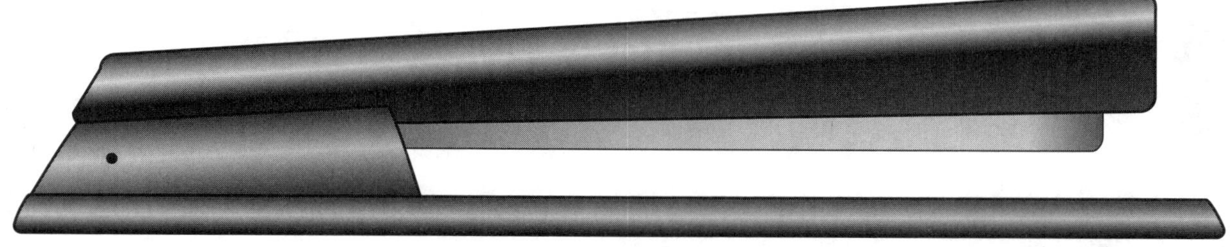

Part A About how long is this stapler?

Answer ____________________

Think of an object that is about 1 centimeter long.

Part B Explain how you made your estimate.

____

____

____

____

Lesson 3

Measuring Lengths

2.MD.1, 2.MD.2

Other tools for measuring length are:

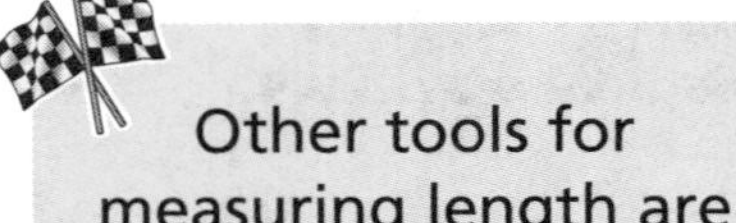

yardstick

meter stick

measuring tape

An inch (in.) is a customary unit of measurement.

Use inches to measure small things.

A centimeter (cm) is a metric unit of measurement.

Use centimeters to measure small things.

An inch is longer than a centimeter.

1 inch

1 centimeter

A **ruler** is a tool to measure length. It usually shows inches or centimeters.

An **inch ruler** is marked in inches. To use a ruler, line up the object with the left end of the ruler. Find the other end of the object. Look at the number on the ruler closest to the end of the object.

How many inches long is this key?

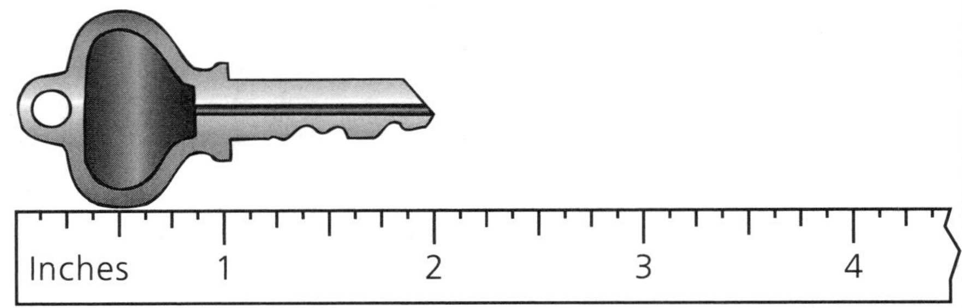

This key is 2 inches long.

A **centimeter ruler** is marked in centimeters. Use a centimeter ruler the same way you use an inch ruler.

How many centimeters long is this key?

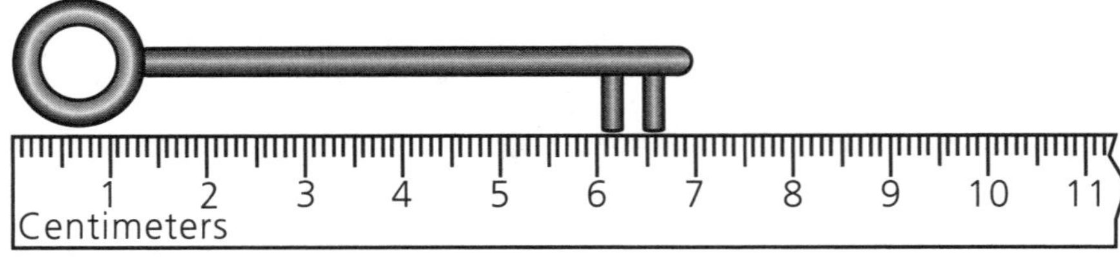

This key is 7 centimeters long.

Read each problem. Circle the letter of the best answer.

SAMPLE Use your inch ruler to help you answer this question.

Which of these lines is 3 inches long?

A 

B

C

D 

The correct answer is D. Use your inch ruler. Measure each line. Line up the end of the line with the end of the ruler. Look at the other end of the line. Find the number on the ruler closest to where the other end stops. The line in choice D is 3 inches long.

1 Use your centimeter ruler to help you answer this question.

Mr. Young wore this name tag at a party.

What is the length of this name tag?

A 5 cm

B 6 cm

C 8 cm

D 9 cm

2 Jay drew a line that was 10 inches long. Lara drew a line that was 10 centimeters long. What is true?

A Jay's line is longer than Lara's line.

B Lara's line is longer than Jay's line.

C Both lines are the same length.

D You cannot tell how long the lines are.

3 Use your inch ruler to help you answer this question.

How long is this piece of wire?

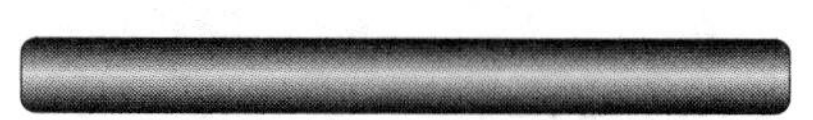

A 1 inch

B 2 inches

C 3 inches

D 4 inches

Read each problem. Write your answer.

SAMPLE Isaiah measures a stick with his inch ruler. Then he measures it with his centimeter ruler. The stick is 12 inches long. What is true about the stick's length in centimeters?

Answer ______________________________

The stick's length is more than 12 centimeters. Centimeters are smaller than inches. You have to use more centimeters than inches to measure the same length. The stick is 12 inches long. So it will be longer than 12 centimeters.

4 Use your inch ruler to help you answer this question.

How long is this chain?

Answer ____________________

5 Use your centimeter ruler to help you answer this question.

What is the length of this pencil?

Answer ______________________________

6 Use your centimeter ruler to help you answer this question.

Draw a line that is 8 centimeters long in the space below.

Read each problem. Write your answer to each part.

7 Use your centimeter ruler and your inch ruler to help you answer this question.

Brigit measured the length of her hair barrette twice.

Part A What is the length of the barrette to the nearest inch? What is the length of the barrette to the nearest centimeter?

Inches __________

Centimeters __________

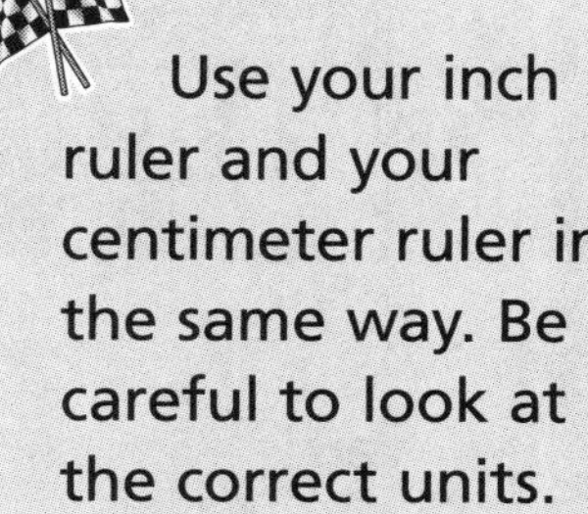

Use your inch ruler and your centimeter ruler in the same way. Be careful to look at the correct units.

Part B Explain why the numbers of units are not the same.

____

____

____

8 Use your inch ruler and your centimeter ruler to help you answer this question.

Dae-Ho needs a piece of string that is 5 inches long.

Part A In the space below, draw a line that is 5 inches long.

Part B Is the line you drew more than or less than 12 centimeters long?

Answer ____________________

Lesson 4

Adding and Subtracting Lengths

2.MD.4, 2.MD.5

Use a ruler to measure length.

Customary units of length:

inches
feet
yards
miles

Metric units of length:

centimeters
meters
kilometers

Use these steps to solve a problem.

1. Read the problem carefully.
2. Think about the problem.
3. Solve the problem.
4. Check your answer.

Sometimes you can make a drawing to help you solve a problem.

You can measure objects to find how much longer one is than the other. Measure both objects. Then subtract.

How much longer is line A than line B?

A

B

Use an inch ruler to measure these two lines. Line A is 5 inches long. Line B is 2 inches long.

Subtract to find the difference: 5 − 2 = 3 inches

Line A is 3 inches longer than line B.

Sometimes you need to add and subtract lengths to solve problems. Read the problem carefully. Then decide how you will solve it.

Malik has a piece of rope that is 4 feet long. He has a second piece of rope. He has 15 feet of rope in all. How long is the second piece of rope?

You can write a number sentence to help you solve this problem.

4 feet + □ feet = 15 feet

Solve the equation. Find the unknown number.

Subtract: 15 − 4 = 11

So □ = 11 because 4 + 11 = 15.

The second piece of rope is 11 feet long.

Read each problem. Circle the letter of the best answer.

SAMPLE Miss Bender has two pieces of cloth. One piece is 12 feet long. The other piece is 18 feet long. Miss Bender sews the two pieces together. What is the total length of the cloth?

A 12 feet **B** 20 feet **C** 30 feet **D** 40 feet

The correct answer is C. To find the total length, add the two lengths: 12 + 18 = 30 feet. The cloth will be 30 feet long after Miss Bender sews the pieces together.

1 Use your centimeter ruler to help you answer this question.

Look at these two pins.

How much longer is pin B than pin A?

A 2 centimeters

B 3 centimeters

C 6 centimeters

D 9 centimeters

2 Mr. Rossi has two fences. He has 46 yards of fence in all. One fence is 32 yards long. How long is the other fence?

A 14 yards

B 16 yards

C 78 yards

D 80 yards

3 Use your inch ruler to help you answer this question.

Look at these two nails.

A
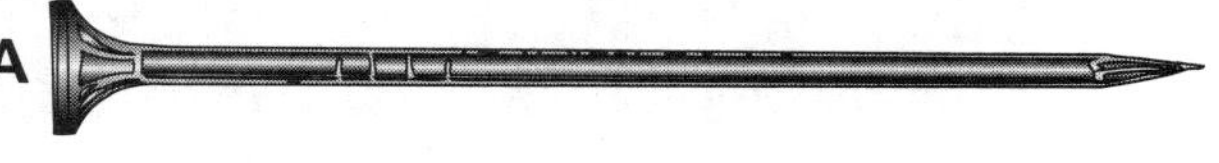

B
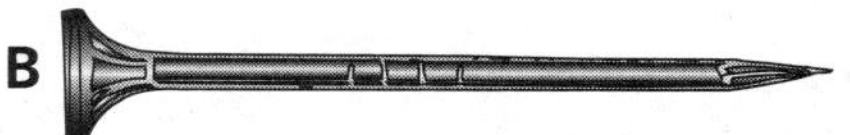

How much longer is nail A than nail B?

A 5 inches **C** 2 inches

B 4 inches **D** 1 inch

4 Kayla hung paper streamers for a party. One roll of streamers was 25 meters long. The other roll was 62 meters long. What was the total length of the streamers Kayla hung?

A 25 meters

B 62 meters

C 87 meters

D 98 meters

Read each problem. Write your answer.

SAMPLE Use your centimeter ruler to help you answer this question.

Luis has these two pieces of craft sticks.

A

B

How much longer is stick B than stick A?

Answer ______________________

Stick B is 5 centimeters longer than stick A. Measure both sticks using your centimeter ruler. The length of stick A is 4 centimeters. The length of stick B is 9 centimeters. Subtract to find the difference: 9 − 4 = 5 centimeters.

5 Mr. Gardner needs a wood board that is 52 inches long. He buys a wood board that is 60 inches long. How much does Mr. Gardner need to cut off the wood board he bought?

Answer ______________________

6 Use your inch ruler to help you answer this question.

Uri measures these two worms.

A

B

How much longer is worm A than worm B?

Answer ______________________

Read each problem. Write your answer to each part.

7 Mrs. Colatta has two pieces of pipe. She will put the pieces together to make one pipe. The total length must be 85 inches. One piece of pipe is 38 inches long.

Part A How long is the other piece of pipe?

Answer ____________________

What number sentence shows this situation?

Part B Explain how you found your answer.

____

____

____

____

8 Use your centimeter ruler to help you answer this question.

Part A In the space below, draw a line that is 4 centimeters long. Draw a second line that is 10 centimeters longer than the first line.

Part B How long is the second line?

Answer ______________________________

LESSON 5

Time

2.MD.7

Some clocks are analog. They show time with hands.

Some clocks are digital. They show time with numbers.

Times between 12:00 midnight and 12:00 noon are A.M. times. These are morning times.

Times between 12:00 noon and 12:00 midnight are P.M. times. These are afternoon and evening times.

Use a **clock** to tell time. There are two hands on a clock. The long hand points to the minutes after the hour. It is the minute hand. The short hand points to the hour. It is the hour hand.

What times do these clocks show?

The hour hand points to the 3. The minute hand points to the 12. This clock shows 3:00.

The hour hand is between 3 and 4. The minute hand points to the 6. This clock shows 3:30.

There are 60 minutes in 1 hour. All the way around the clock is 1 hour. The numbers are 5 minutes apart.

What time does this clock show?

The hour hand is just past the 7. So the hour is 7. The minute hand points to the 4. Count by 5's: 5, 10, 15, 20. So the minutes are 20. This clock shows 7:20.

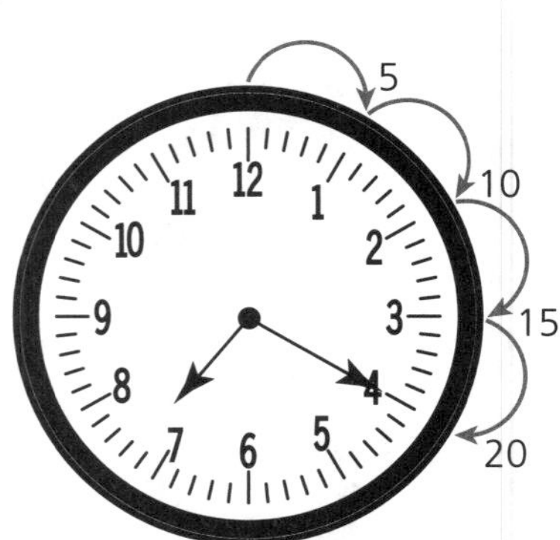

Read each problem. Circle the letter of the best answer.

SAMPLE April gets up at half past 7 in the morning. Which clock shows half past 7?

A 

B 7:00

C 7:30

D 7:45

The correct answer is C. There are 60 minutes in an hour. There are 30 minutes in a half hour. "Half past" means a half hour, or 30 minutes, past. So half past 7 is written as 7:30 with numbers.

1 Which clock shows 1:50?

A 

C 

B 

D 

2 Jin comes home from school at 3 o'clock in the afternoon. Which of these is 3 o'clock in the afternoon?

A 3:00 P.M.

B 3:30 P.M.

C 3:00 A.M.

D 3:30 A.M.

3 What time does this clock show?

A 2:35

B 2:40

C 8:05

D 8:10

4 Cameron ate a snack at quarter of eleven. Which clock shows this time?

A 

C 

B 11:15

D 

Read each problem. Write your answer.

SAMPLE An airplane leaves at the time shown on this clock.

What time does the airplane leave?

Answer ___________

The plane leaves at 9:15. The short hand is the hour hand. It is just a little past the 9. The long hand is the minute hand. It is pointing to the 3. Count by 5's: 5, 10, 15. The minutes are 15. The time is 9:15.

5 Samira went to the park at 12:35. Draw hands on this clock to show 12:35.

6 Dan goes to hockey practice every morning. He goes at the time shown on this clock.

What time does Dan go to hockey practice? Include A.M. or P.M.

Answer ______________________

Read each problem. Write your answer to each part.

7 Nick has a karate lesson on Friday afternoon. His lesson starts at the time shown on this clock.

What part of the day has A.M. times? What part of the day has P.M. times?

Part A What time does Nick's lesson start? Include A.M. or P.M.

Answer ____________________

Part B Explain how you knew if the time was A.M. or P.M.

____

____

____

8 Rachel started her homework at half past 5.

Part A Write this time on the digital clock below.

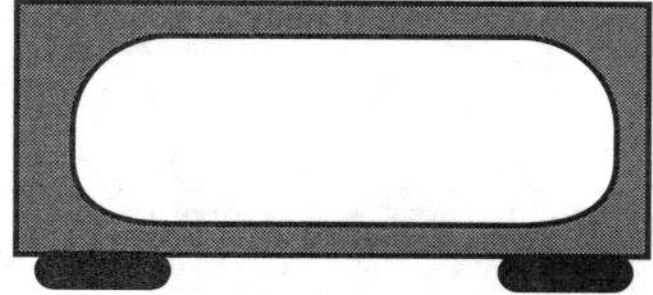

Part B Draw the hands on the clock to show this time.

LESSON 6

Money

2.MD.8

The $ symbol means "dollars." Put it before dollar amounts.

$3.00 $4.25

The ¢ symbol means "cents." Put it after cent amounts.

54¢ 78¢

You can also write cent amounts with the $ symbol.

$0.25 = 25¢ = 25 cents

When you count money, start with the paper bills. Then count the coins from the greatest value to the least value.

Some **money** is paper bills. Some money is coins. Each type of bill and coin is worth a certain amount.

One-dollar bill
$1.00

Quarter
$0.25 25¢

Dime
$0.10 10¢

Nickel
$0.05 5¢

Penny
$0.01 1¢

Count the value of bills and coins to find how much money.

Abel has this money. How much money does he have?

There are 2 one-dollar bills, 1 quarter, and 1 dime.

A one-dollar bill is worth $1.00. There are two bills:
$1.00 + $1.00 = $2.00
A quarter is worth 25 cents. There is one quarter: $0.25
A dime is worth 10 cents. There is one dime: $0.10
Add: $2.00 + $0.25 = $2.25, $2.25 + $0.10 = $2.35

Abel has $2.35.

Read each problem. Circle the letter of the best answer.

SAMPLE Ella has two dimes and three nickels. How much money does Ella have?

A 23¢ **B** 35¢ **C** 40¢ **D** 80¢

The correct answer is B. A dime is worth 10¢. A nickel is worth 5¢. There are two dimes: 10¢ + 10¢ = 20¢. There are three nickels: 5¢ + 5¢ + 5¢ = 15¢. Add: 20¢ + 15¢ = 35¢.

1 Dean used the money below to buy a sandwich.

How much did the sandwich cost?

A $3.03 **C** $3.30

B $3.15 **D** $3.75

2 Keisha paid for a sweater. She got two one-dollar bills, a dime, and four pennies back. How much did Keisha get back?

A $2.05 **C** $2.14

B $2.09 **D** $2.29

3 Deb spent one quarter, six dimes, and one nickel at a yard sale. How much did Deb spend?

A 41¢ **C** 90¢

B 65¢ **D** $1.65

4 Jose found these coins in his pocket.

How much money did Jose find in his pocket?

A 36¢ **C** 76¢

B 51¢ **D** 80¢

5 Sally has four quarters, three dimes, and one penny in her purse. She has two dimes and eight pennies in her wallet. How much does Sally have in all?

A $0.69 **C** $1.34

B $0.84 **D** $1.59

Read each problem. Write your answer.

SAMPLE DeShawn's mom paid him this money for helping to wash the car.

How much did DeShawn's mom pay him?

Answer __________

DeShawn's mom paid him $5.00. First count the bills. There are four one-dollar bills. This is worth $4.00. Then count the coins. There are four quarters. A quarter is worth 25¢. Four quarters make $1.00. Add the two amounts: $4.00 + $1.00 = $5.00.

6 There were three quarters, five dimes, and two pennies in a piggy bank. There were seven dimes, three nickels, and three pennies in a desk drawer. How much money was there in all? Show your work.

Answer __________

7 Anya bought a birthday card for her grandmother. She paid for the card with this money.

How much did the birthday card cost?

Answer __________

Read the problem. Write your answer to each part.

8 Ricardo has these coins.

Part A What is the value of these coins?

Answer __________

Count the coins with the largest values first.

Part B Ricardo finds two one-dollar bills and one nickel in his room. How much money does he have now? Explain how you found your answer.

____

____

____

____

REVIEW

Measurement

Read each problem. Circle the letter of the best answer.

1 Use your inch ruler to help you answer this question.

What is the length of this leaf?

A 1 inch **C** 3 inches

B 2 inches **D** 4 inches

2 What time is shown on this clock?

A 12:25 **C** 5:00

B 1:25 **D** 5:05

3 Which is a good estimate of the height of a flagpole?

A 1 centimeter **C** 1 meter

B 8 centimeters **D** 8 meters

4 Liam cuts a piece of paper that is 8 feet long. He wants to add another piece of paper to make a sign 12 feet long. How long must the second piece of paper be?

A 2 feet **C** 6 feet

B 4 feet **D** 8 feet

5 Yolanda spent five one-dollar bills and two quarters at the store. How much did Yolanda spend?

A \$5.02 **C** \$5.20

B \$5.10 **D** \$5.50

6 Look at these two paper clips.

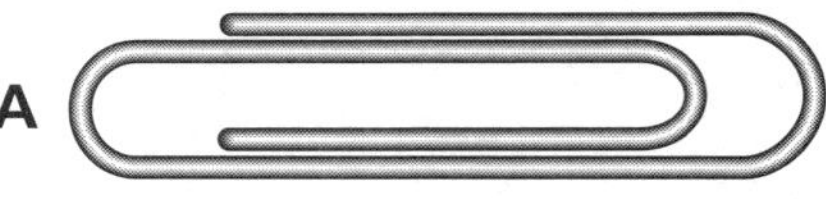

How much longer is paper clip A than paper clip B?

A 1 centimeter **C** 3 centimeters

B 2 centimeters **D** 4 centimeters

Read each problem. Write your answer.

7 Andy measured a piece of yarn. The piece of yarn was 18 inches long. Andy says the piece of yarn is also 18 centimeters long. Is Andy correct? Explain why or why not.

____

____

8 Use your centimeter ruler to help you answer this question.

How long is this comb?

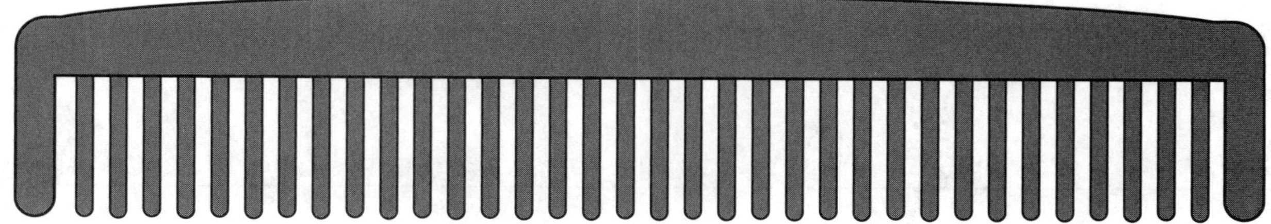

Answer ____________________

9 Michelle spent some of her birthday money. She had this money left.

How much money did Michelle have left?

Answer __________

10 Natka has two rolls of tape. One roll has 30 yards of tape. The other roll has 46 yards of tape. What is the total length of the tape Natka has?

Answer ____________________

Read each problem. Write your answer to each part.

11 Suki's soccer game starts at 10 o'clock in the morning.

Part A Draw hands on this clock to show the time that Suki's game starts.

Part B Is this time an A.M. time or a P.M. time? Explain how you know.

____

____

12 Look at this marker.

Part A About how many inches long is this marker?

Answer ___________

Part B Explain how you found your answer.

____

____

____

Unit 6

Data

- **Lesson 1 Number Lines** reviews how to find points on a number line and how to use a number line to add and subtract.
- **Lesson 2 Bar Graphs** reviews how to read and make a bar graph.
- **Lesson 3 Pictographs** reviews how to read and make a pictograph.
- **Lesson 4 Line Plots** reviews how to read and make a line plot.

Lesson 1

Number Lines

2.MD.6

Every number has a place on a number line. This place is called a **point.**

Always read a number line carefully. Sometimes the numbers do not count by 1's. They may count by 2's, 5's, or any other number.

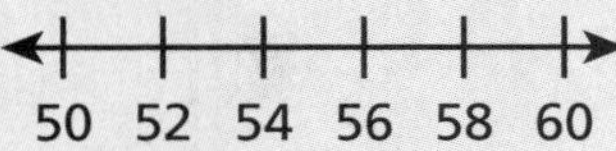

A number line does not always start with 0. It can start and end with any number.

To add, move to the right on a number line.

To subtract, move to the left on a number line.

A **number line** shows numbers in order from least to greatest. Each number is a certain distance from 0.

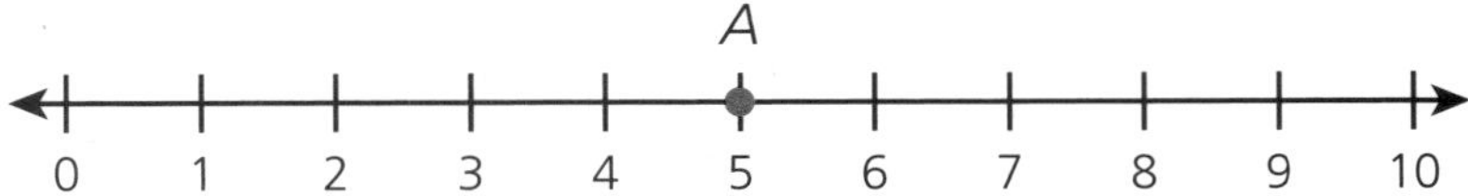

Point *A* is at 5 on this number line. Point *A* is 5 units from 0.

Use a number line to help you add and subtract.

Find the sum 9 + 5 on this number line.

Find 9 on the number line. Count up 5 marks from 9.

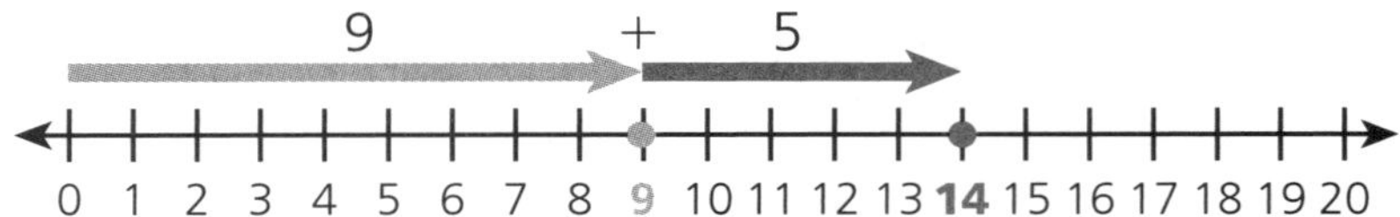

Look at where you stopped on the number line: 14

So, 9 + 5 = 14.

Find 18 − 6 on this number line.

Start at 18 on the number line. Count back 6 marks.

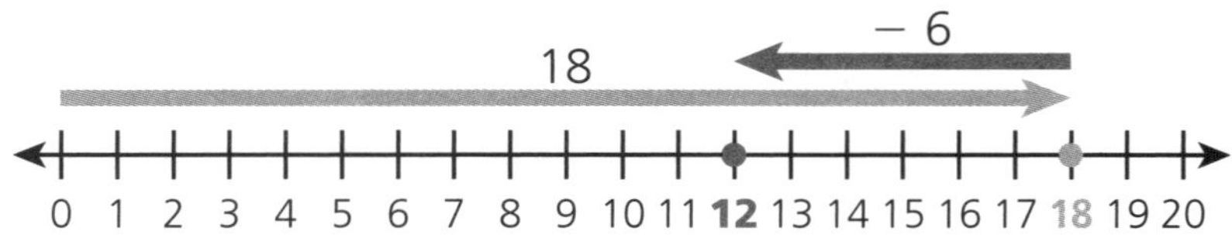

Look at where you stopped on the number line: 12

So, 18 − 6 = 12.

Read each problem. Circle the letter of the best answer.

SAMPLE How many units from 0 is point *A* on this number line?

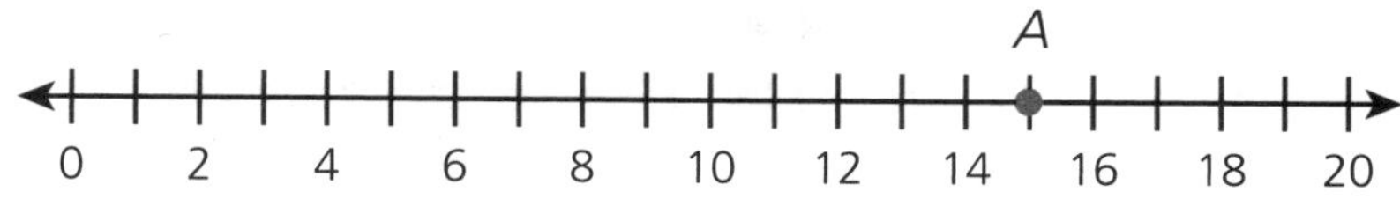

A 5 **B** 10 **C** 15 **D** 16

The correct answer is C. Look at the number line carefully. It starts at 0. It ends at 20. The marks are labeled by 2's. Only the even numbers are labeled. Point *A* is between 14 and 16, so it is at 15 on this number line. It is 15 units from 0.

1 Which number line shows 13 + 8?

A

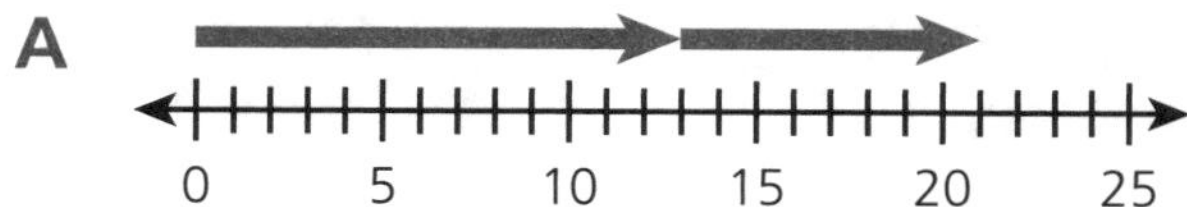

B

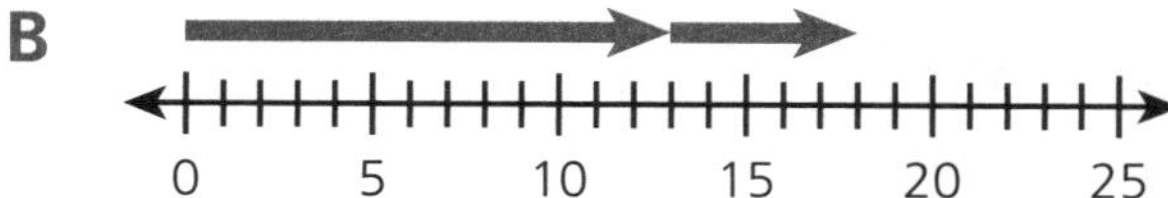

C

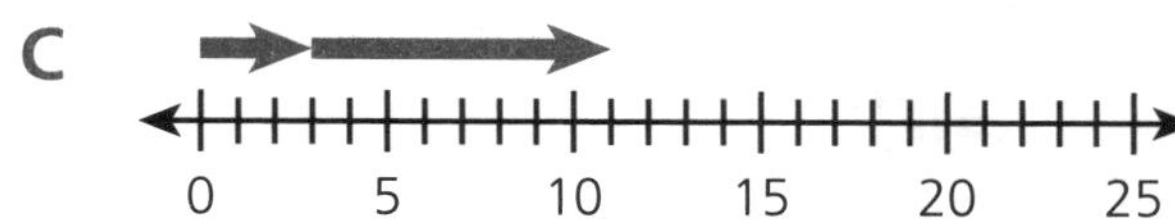

D

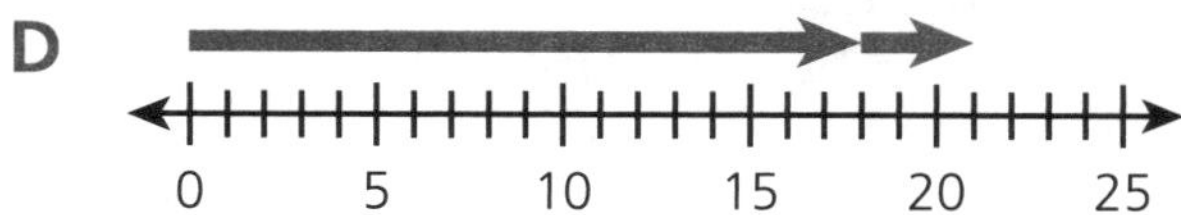

2 Look at this number line.

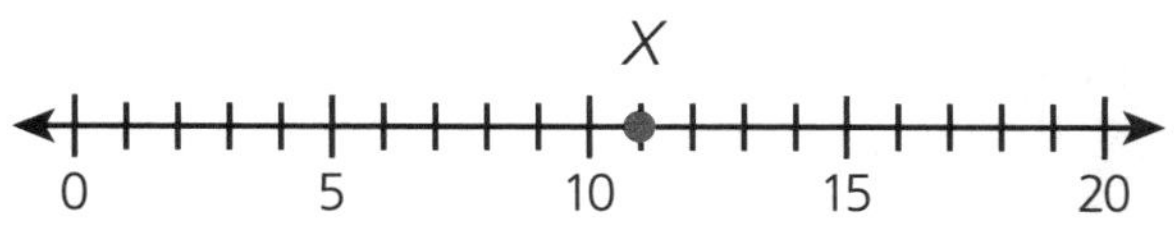

How many units from 0 is point *X* on this number line?

A 5 **C** 11

B 6 **D** 19

3 Look at the number line below.

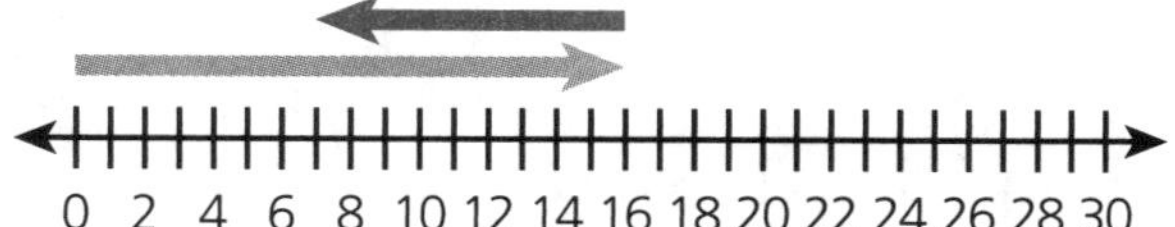

What number sentence does this number line show?

A 16 + 9 = 25

B 16 + 10 = 26

C 26 − 9 = 17

D 16 − 9 = 7

4 Look at the number line below.

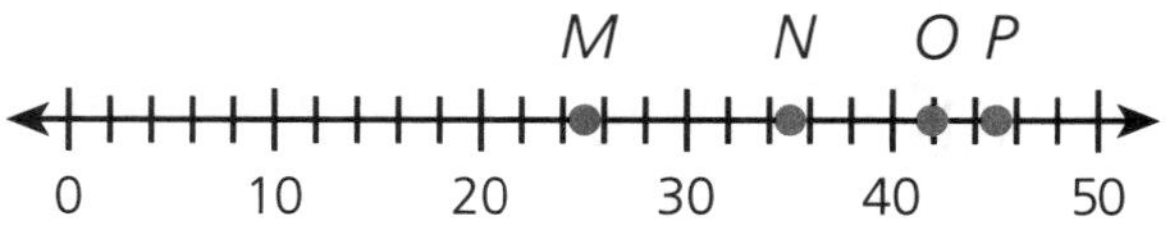

Which point is 35 units from 0 on the number line?

A point *M* **C** point *O*

B point *N* **D** point *P*

Read each problem. Write your answer.

SAMPLE Look at the number line below.

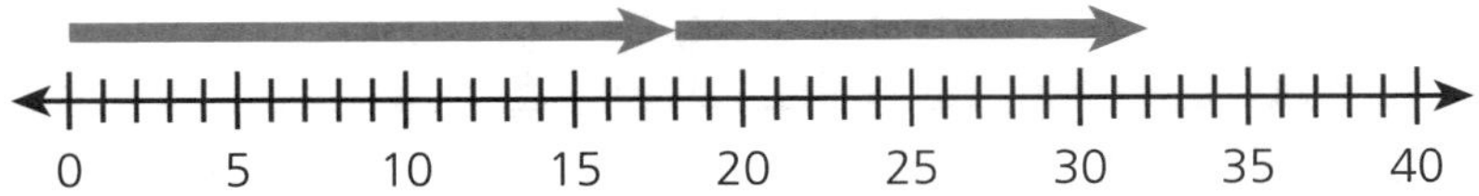

What number sentence does the number line show?

Answer ____________________________

The number line shows two arrows. Both point to the right. So it shows an addition number sentence. The first arrow goes from 0 to 18, so it shows 18. The second arrow goes from 18 to 32. This is 14 units more than 18. So the number sentence is 18 + 14 = 32.

5 Find 53 − 12. Show your work on the number line.

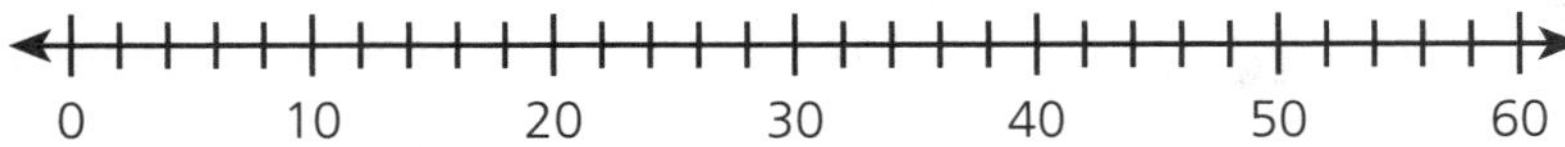

Answer __________

6 On a number line, point *G* is 19 units from 0. Plot point *G* on this number line.

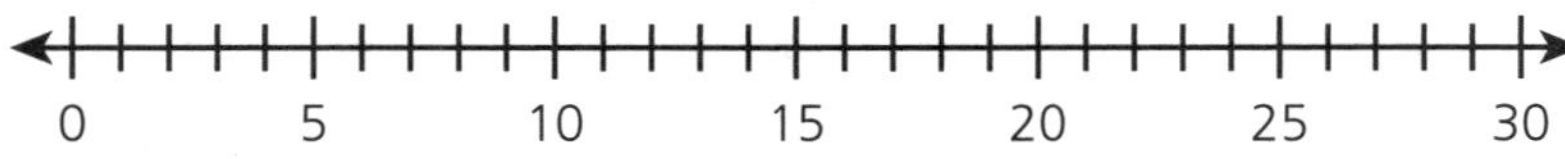

7 Explain how you can use this number line to find 24 + 15.

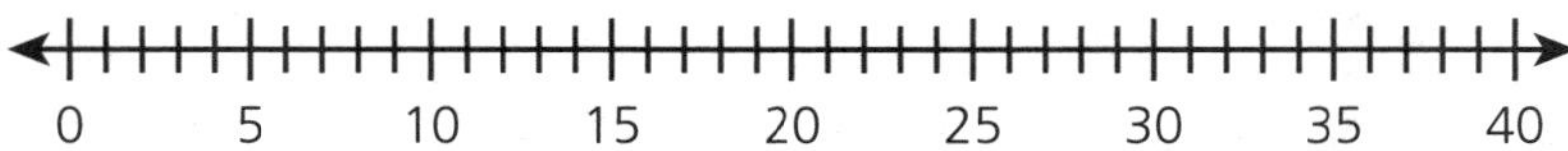

____

____

Read the problem. Write your answer to each part.

8 Point Y is at 64 on the number line below.

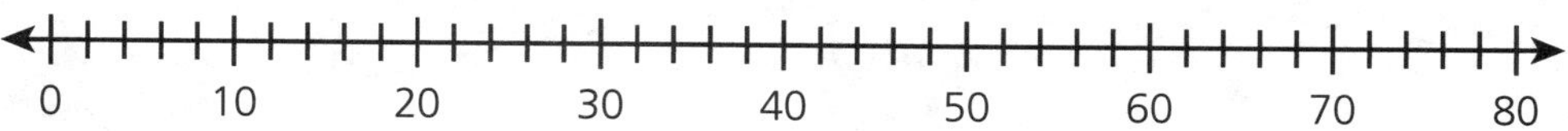

Part A Plot point Y on the number line above.

Part B Use the number line to find the sum of 64 and 14. Explain what you did.

____

____

____

____

____

To find a sum, do you move to the right or the left on the number line?

LESSON 2

Bar Graphs

2.MD.10

The **scale** is the numbers along the side or across the bottom of a bar graph. Read the numbers carefully. Sometimes the scale counts by 1's. Sometimes it counts by 2's, 5's, or another number.

The bars on a bar graph can go up.

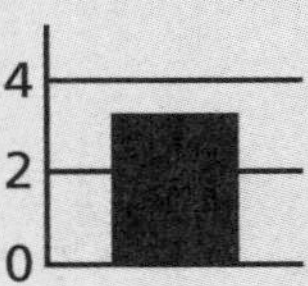

The bars on a bar graph can go across.

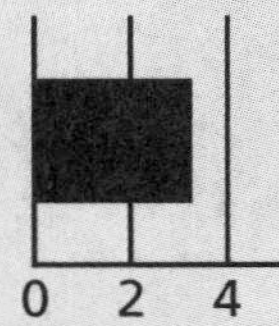

You can make a bar graph. Look at data in a table. Draw a bar for each number.

Bar graphs use bars to show data. **Data** is information. Read the title and the labels on the bar graph. They help you understand what it is about.

Here's how to read a bar graph. Find the bar that shows the data you want. Look from the end of the bar to the scale. Read the number on the scale where the bar ends.

Eli counted the number of tomatoes he picked each day. He made this bar graph.

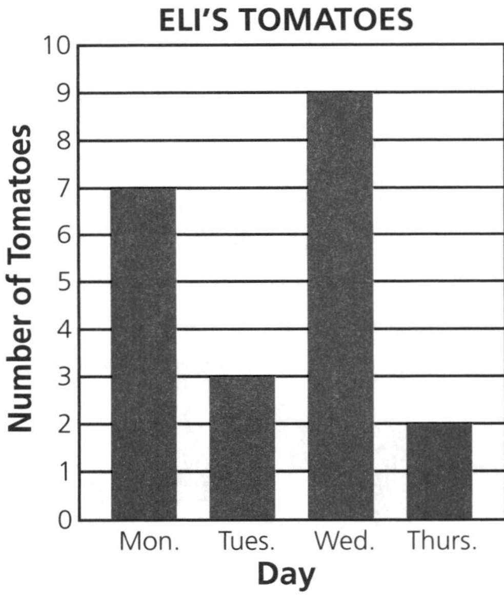

How many tomatoes did Eli pick on Wednesday?

Find the bar labeled Wednesday. Find the top of the bar. Then move across to the number on the scale: 9

Eli picked 9 tomatoes on Wednesday.

Read each problem. Circle the letter of the best answer.

SAMPLE How many times did Aiko go sledding in January?

A 4 **C** 9

B 8 **D** 10

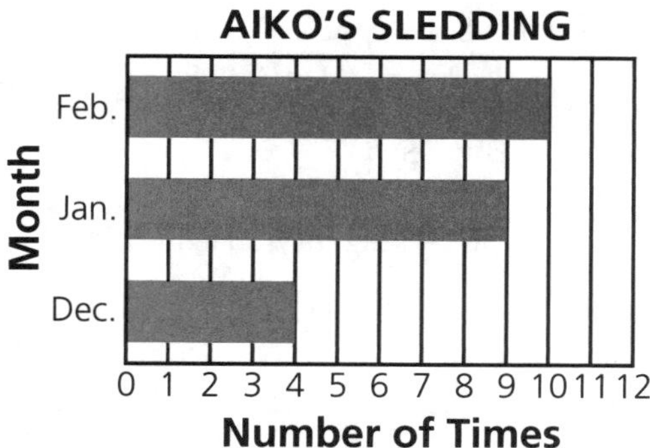

The correct answer is C. Find the bar for January. It is the middle bar. Look across until you find the end of the bar. Then look down at the scale. The bar stops at 9 on the scale. So the bar shows she went sledding 9 times in January.

1 Which bar graph shows the data in this table?

CANNED FOOD COLLECTION

Day	Number of Cans
Thursday	12
Friday	18
Saturday	14

A

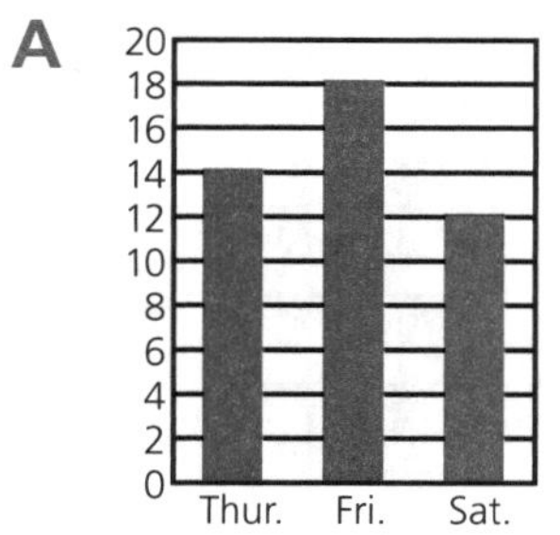

C

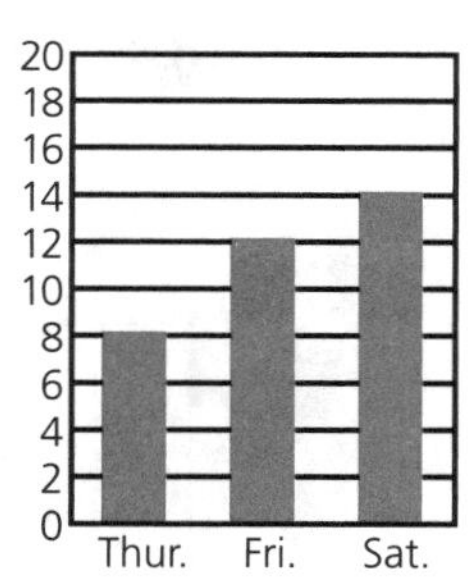

B

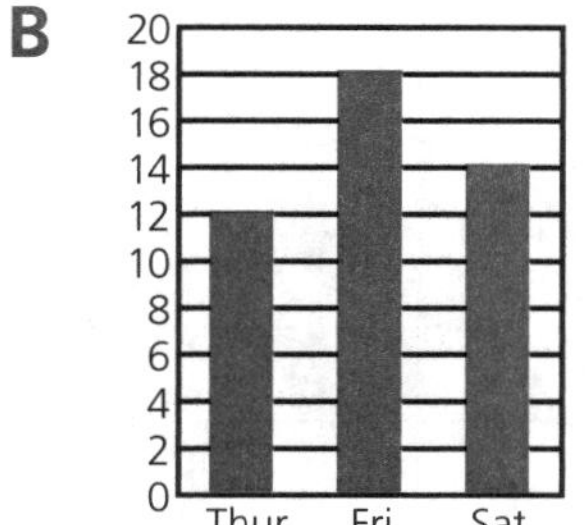

D

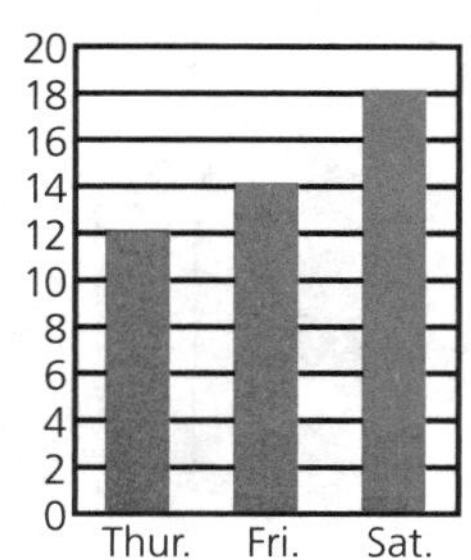

Use this bar graph to answer questions 2 and 3.

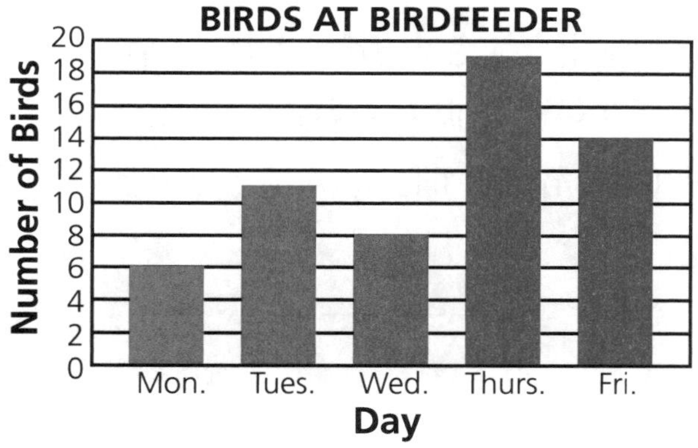

2 On which day were the most birds at the birdfeeder?

A Tuesday **C** Thursday

B Wednesday **D** Friday

3 How many more birds were at the feeder Tuesday than Wednesday?

A 3 **C** 11

B 4 **D** 19

Read each problem. Write your answer.

SAMPLE This tally chart shows some students' favorite ice cream flavors.

Use this tally chart to make a bar graph.

FAVORITE ICE CREAM

Flavor	Number of Students
Chocolate	~~////~~ ///
Vanilla	~~////~~
Strawberry	//

Each tally means 1 student. Count the number of tallies beside each flavor. There are 8 tallies for chocolate. There are 5 tallies for vanilla. There are 2 tallies for strawberry. Draw bars for these flavors that show these numbers. The bar graph will look like this:

4 This bar graph shows the types of flowers in a vase.

How many lilies are in the vase?

Answer ____________

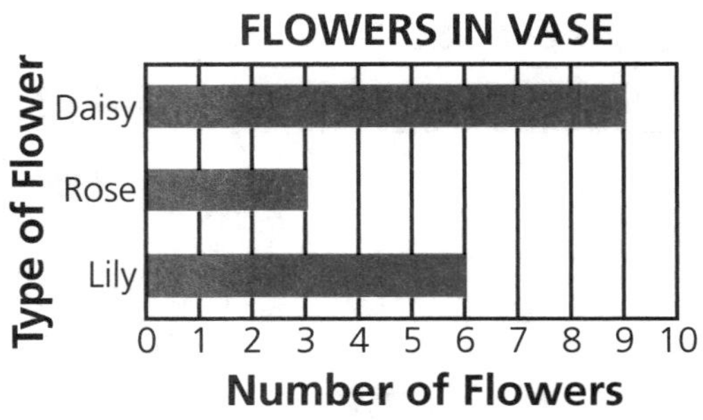

5 This table shows the types of fruit in a basket.

FRUIT IN BASKET

Fruit	Number of Pieces
Apple	3
Orange	7
Banana	4

Make a bar graph on the grid at the right. Show the data in the table.

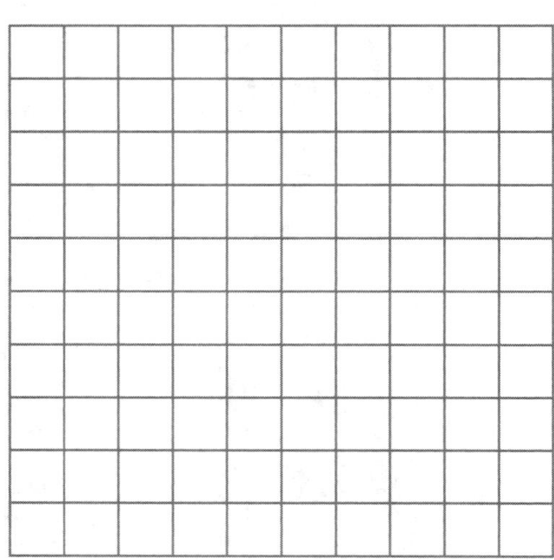

Read the problem. Write your answer to each part.

6 Look at the tally chart below. It shows the number of horses on four farms.

HORSES ON FARMS

Farm	Number of Horses
A	~~||||~~ ||||
B	~~||||~~ ~~||||~~ ||||
C	||||
D	~~||||~~ ||

Part A Make a bar graph on the grid below. Show the data in the table.

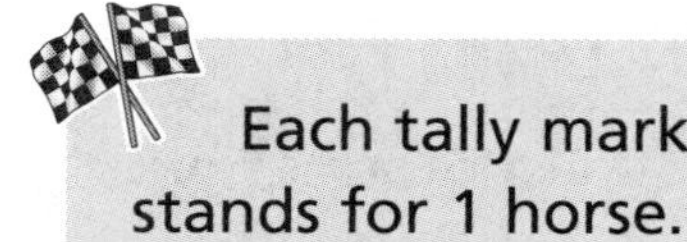

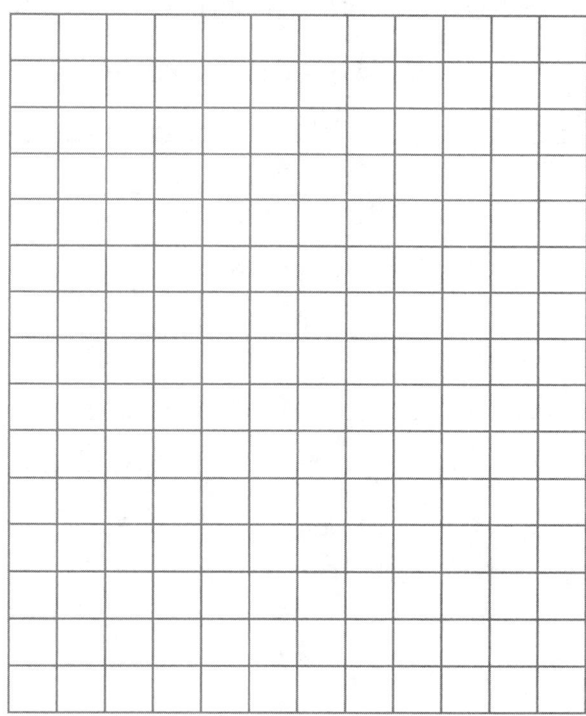

Part B How many more horses are on farm B than on farm C?

Answer ___________

Lesson 3

Pictographs

2.MD.10

A pictograph is sometimes called a picture graph.

Data is information.

Read the key carefully. A symbol can stand for any number. It might be worth 1, 2, 5, 10, or another number.

You can skip count symbols by the symbol value.

If ★ = 2 stars, skip count by 2's.

★ ★ ★ ★
2, 4, 6, 8

You can add the values of symbols.

If ● = 5 flowers, add.

● ● ●
5 + 5 + 5 = 15

Pictographs use pictures or symbols to show data. A **key** tells you the value of each symbol.

Here's how to read a pictograph. Find the row that shows the data you want. Count the symbols in that row. Remember to look at the key to see the value of the symbol.

Three friends have stamp collections. This pictograph shows how many stamps each person has.

STAMP COLLECTIONS

Name	Number of Stamps
Irina	♥ ♥ ♥ ♥ ♥ ♥ ♥ ♥
Frank	♥ ♥ ♥ ♥ ♥ ♥ ♥ ♥ ♥ ♥ ♥ ♥ ♥
Reggie	♥ ♥ ♥ ♥ ♥ ♥ ♥

Key: ♥ = 2 stamps

How many stamps does Reggie have?

Find the row for Reggie on the pictograph.
Look at the key. The key says that each symbol stands for 2 stamps. Count the symbols by 2's: 2, 4, 6, 8, 10, 12, 14

Reggie has 14 stamps.

Read each problem. Circle the letter of the best answer.

SAMPLE Alaina is making a picture graph. Each symbol means 5 objects. How many symbols does she need to show 25 objects?

A 6 **B** 5 **C** 4 **D** 3

The correct answer is B. You can skip count to find the number of symbols. Skip count by 5's until you get to 25: 5, 10, 15, 20, 25. You said 5 numbers, so you need 5 symbols.

Use this pictograph to answer questions 1 and 2.

AMUSEMENT PARK RIDE LINES

Ride	Number of People
Carousel	☺☺☺☺☺
Roller Coaster	☺☺☺☺☺☺☺☺
Giant Swing	☺☺☺
Water Slide	☺☺☺☺☺☺☺☺☺

Key: ☺ = 10 people

1 How many people are in line for the Giant Swing?

A 3

B 15

C 30

D 60

2 Which ride has the longest line?

A Carousel

B Roller Coaster

C Giant Swing

D Water Slide

3 Look at the data in this table.

MY MUSIC

Type of Music	Number of Downloads
Rock	7
Jazz	2
Pop	6

Which pictograph shows the data in this table?

A **MY MUSIC**

Music Type	Number of Downloads
Rock	◆◆◆◆◆◆◆
Jazz	◆◆◆◆◆◆
Pop	◆◆

Key: ◆ = 1 DL

B **MY MUSIC**

Music Type	Number of Downloads
Rock	◆◆◆◆◆◆◆
Jazz	◆◆
Pop	◆◆◆◆◆◆

Key: ◆ = 1 DL

C **MY MUSIC**

Music Type	Number of Downloads
Rock	◆◆
Jazz	◆◆◆◆◆◆
Pop	◆◆◆◆◆◆◆

Key: ◆ = 1 DL

D **MY MUSIC**

Music Type	Number of Downloads
Rock	◆◆◆◆◆◆
Jazz	◆◆
Pop	◆◆◆◆◆◆◆

Key: ◆ = 1 DL

Read each problem. Write your answer.

SAMPLE This pictograph shows the number of books three friends read one summer.

How many books did Cesar read?

BOOKS READ

Friend	Number of Books
Jessica	READ READ READ
Neil	READ READ
Cesar	READ READ READ

Key: READ = 4 books

Answer ___________

Cesar read 12 books. The key says that each READ means 4 books. There are 3 symbols beside Cesar's name. Add to find the number of books: 4 + 4 + 4 = 12.

4 Look at the pictograph in the sample problem. Which two friends read the same number of books?

Answer ____

5 This table shows the weather one month.

Use the data in this table to complete this pictograph.

WEATHER ONE MONTH

Weather	Number of Days
Sunny	14
Rainy	6
Cloudy	10

WEATHER ONE MONTH

Weather	Number of Days
Sunny	
Rainy	
Cloudy	

Key: = 2 days

Read the problem. Write your answer to each part.

6 Jane, LaToya, and Keiko are making holiday cards to send to their friends. Jane has made 20 cards. LaToya has made 35 cards. Keiko has made 30 cards.

> How many cards does each symbol stand for? Look at the key.

Part A Complete the pictograph to show the number of cards each friend has made.

HOLIDAY CARDS

Friend	Number of Cards Made

Key: = 5 cards

Part B Explain how you knew the number of symbols to use for each friend.

____

____

____

____

Lesson 4

Line Plots

2.MD.9

Data is information.

Look at the number line carefully. Sometimes the number line does not show all the numbers.

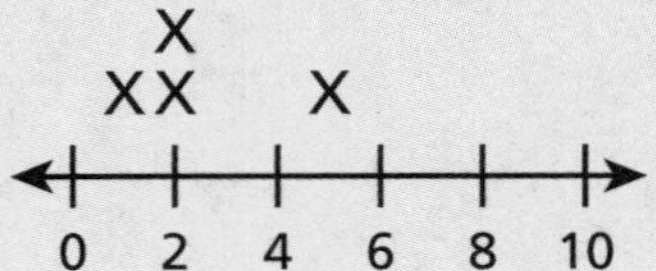

This number line counts by 2's. The X's that are between the marks stand for the odd numbers.

A **line plot** uses X's to show data. Each X is above a number on a number line. The X stands for that number.

Mr. Barton sells canoes. This line plot shows the lengths of 12 canoes.

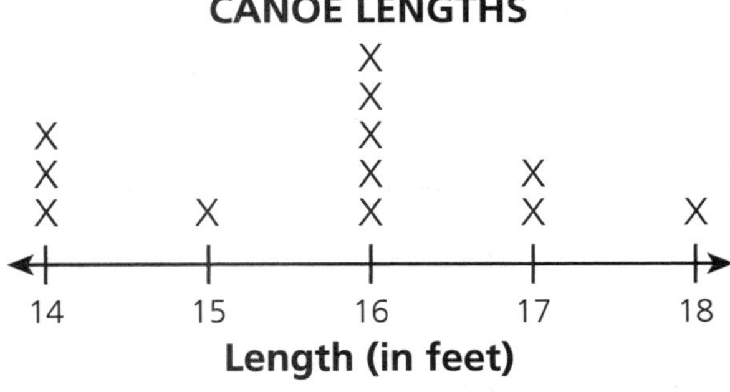

How many canoes are 16 feet long?

Find the mark for 16 feet. Count the number of X's above the mark: 5

So, 5 canoes are 16 feet long.

To make a line plot, first draw a number line. Make sure the number line includes marks for all the data. Make one X for each piece of data.

Read each problem. Circle the letter of the best answer.

SAMPLE This line plot shows the ages of 10 children on a dance team.

How old is the oldest child on the team?

A 6 years old

B 7 years old

C 9 years old

D 10 years old

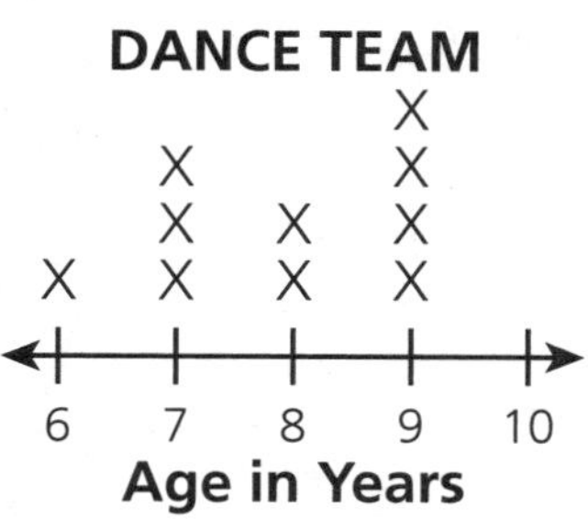

The correct answer is C. Look at the X's above the number line. Each X stands for one child. The number line ends at 10. There are no X's above the 10. The greatest number with an X above it is 9. The oldest child is 9 years old. Actually there are four children who are 9 years old.

Use the line plot in the sample problem to answer questions 1 and 2.

1 How many children are 7 years old?

A 0

B 1

C 2

D 3

2 One more child joins the team. The child is 8 years old. Now how many children on the team are 8 years old?

A 1

B 2

C 3

D 4

3 Mr. Barnes measured the lengths of some snakes. He found that the lengths in centimeters were: 30, 32, 32, 32, 34, 38, 39, 39, 40, 40. Which line plot shows this information?

A

C

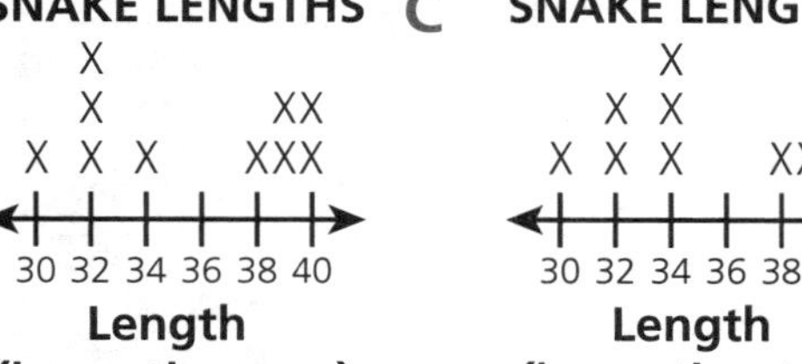

B

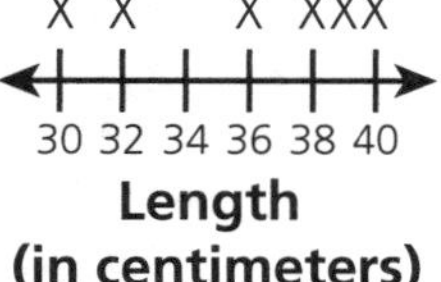

D

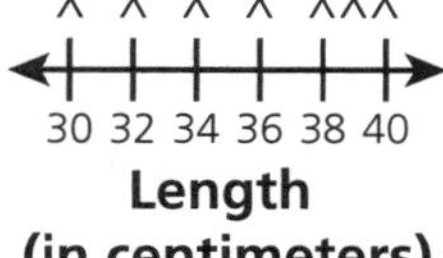

Read each problem. Write your answer.

SAMPLE Some friends went fishing. They caught 10 fish. The lengths, in inches, of the fish were 16, 16, 17, 19, 19, 19, 20, and 22 inches.

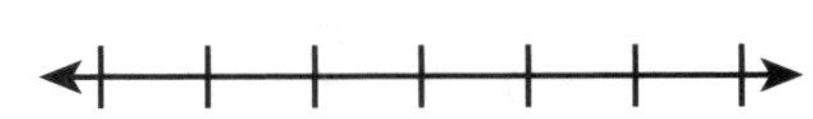

Make a line plot to show this data.

First label the tick marks with the numbers 16, 17, 18, 19, 20, 21, and 22. Then make one X for each fish length. Put the X over the correct number. Remember to label the line plot. Give the line plot a title. The line plot will look like this:

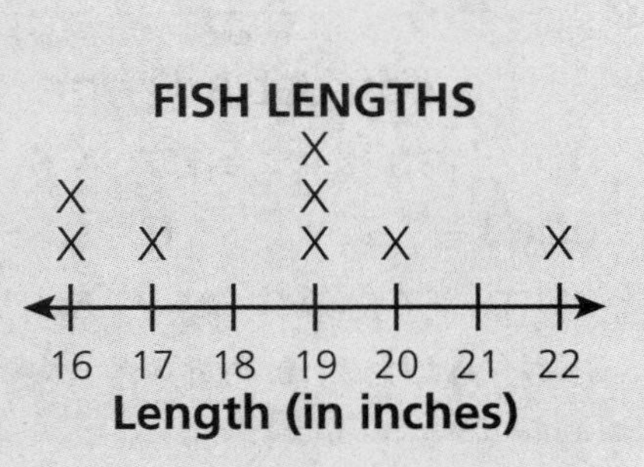

4 This table shows the heights of some students in Todd's class.

STUDENT HEIGHTS

Height (in inches)	Number of Students
47	1
48	0
49	4
50	3
51	2
52	2

Make a line plot to show the data in the table.

Read the problem. Write your answer to each part.

5 Mrs. Witter plants sunflowers in her garden. She measured the heights of her sunflowers. The heights, in inches, of her sunflowers were:

61, 61, 64, 65, 65, 65, 66, 67, 68, 68, 72, 72, 72, 73, 75

Part A Make a line plot to show this data.

Count the tick marks. What number should you start with on the number line?

Part B Explain how you made your line plot.

___

___

___

___

REVIEW

Data

Read each problem. Circle the letter of the best answer.

1 Look at this number line.

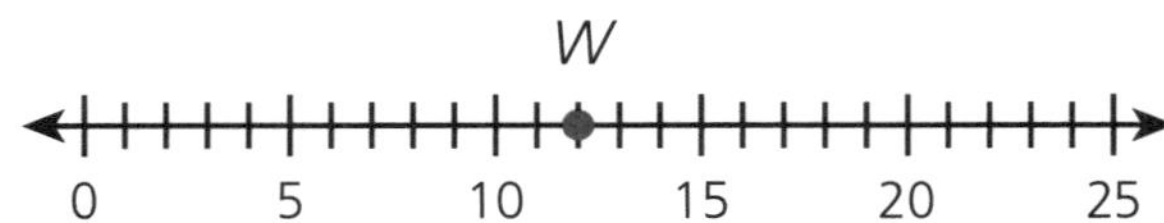

How many units from 0 is point *W*?

A 11 **C** 14

B 12 **D** 15

2 Look at the bar graph below.

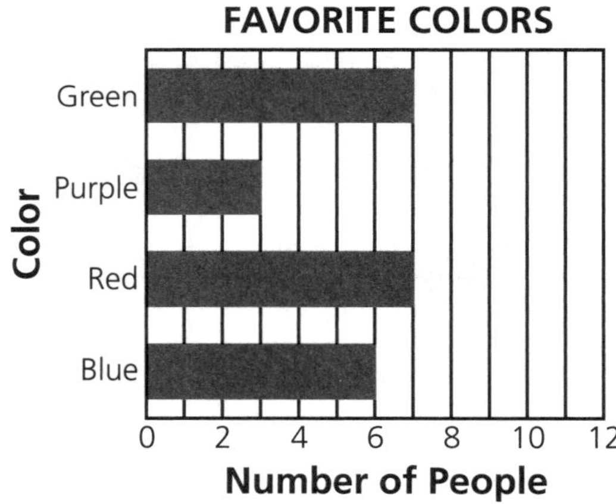

How many people chose red as their favorite color?

A 3 **C** 6

B 5 **D** 7

3 How many jumps were 45 inches long?

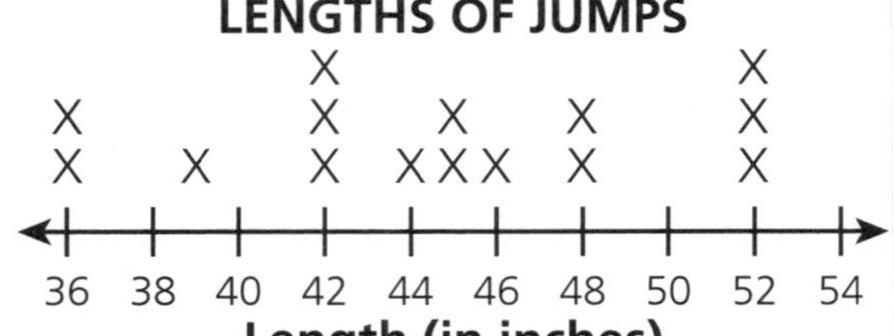

A 0 **C** 2

B 1 **D** 3

4 Dax asked some people to name their favorite sport. This pictograph shows Dax's data.

FAVORITE SPORT

Sport	Number of People
Baseball	☺☺☺☺☺☺☺☺☺
Football	☺☺☺☺☺☺
Basketball	☺☺☺

Key: ☺ = 2 people

How many more people picked baseball than football?

A 3 **C** 9

B 6 **D** 12

Read each problem. Write your answer.

5 Find the sum. Show your work on the number line.

17 + 24 = ☐

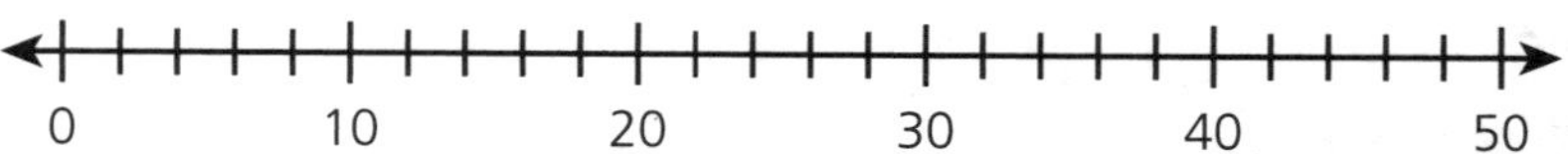

Answer ___________

6 A second-grade class was studying insects. They measured the lengths of 10 insects. The lengths, in centimeters, were 1, 1, 3, 4, 4, 4, 5, 8, 8, and 9. Make a line plot to show this data.

7 Look at the pictograph below. It shows the number of hot dogs, hamburgers, and chicken sandwiches eaten at a picnic.

PICNIC FOOD

Type of Food	Number Eaten
Hot dog	★★★
Hamburger	★★★★★★
Chicken sandwich	★★

Key: ★ = 5 items

How many hot dogs were eaten at the picnic?

Answer ___________

Read the problem. Write your answer to each part.

8 Mr. Cruz's class is selling boxes of candy. Mason sold 14 boxes of candy. Antwon sold 5 boxes of candy. Dave sold 9 boxes of candy.

Part A Make a bar graph to show the number of boxes these three boys sold.

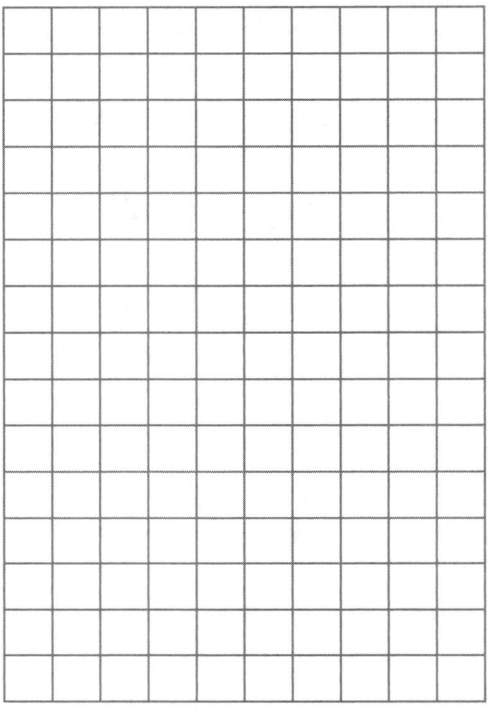

Part B Explain how you made your bar graph.

____

____

____

____

Unit 7

Geometry

- **Lesson 1 Plane Figures** reviews flat figures such as triangles, squares, and pentagons.
- **Lesson 2 Solid Figures** reviews figures like cubes and prisms.
- **Lesson 3 Area** reviews how to divide rectangles into rows of equal-sized squares.
- **Lesson 4 Partitioning Shapes** reviews how to divide circles and rectangles into equal-sized fractional parts.

Lesson 1 Plane Figures

2.G.1

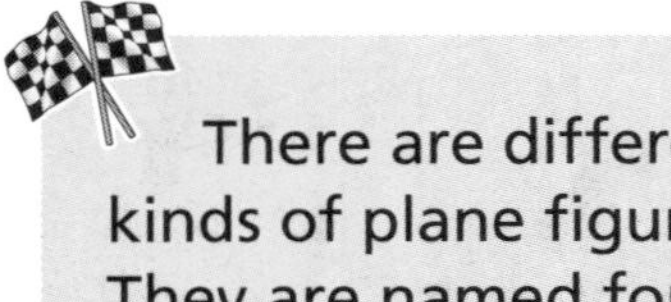

There are different kinds of plane figures. They are named for the number of sides they have.

A plane figure always has the same number of angles as sides.

A square corner is called a right angle.

right angle

There are other kinds of quadrilaterals.

A **parallelogram** has opposite sides that are the same length. It does not always have square corners.

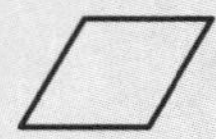

A **rhombus** has four sides that are the same length. It does not always have square corners.

Flat shapes are called **plane figures.**

A **triangle** has three sides. It also has three corners.

Which of these shapes are triangles?

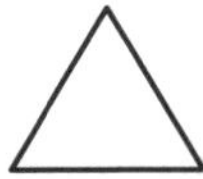  

All the shapes have three sides and three corners. They are all triangles.

A **quadrilateral** has four sides. It also has four corners. Some kinds of quadrilaterals have special names.

What are the names of these quadrilaterals?

A **rectangle** has opposite sides that are the same length. It has square corners.

A **square** is a rectangle with four sides that are the same length.

A **pentagon** has five sides. A **hexagon** has six sides.

Which figure is a pentagon?

A pentagon has five sides. So the figure on the left is a pentagon. The figure on the right has six sides. It is a hexagon.

Read each problem. Circle the letter of the best answer.

SAMPLE Which of these figures is ***not*** a quadrilateral?

A  **B** **C** **D** 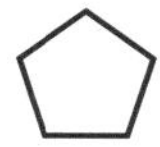

The correct answer is D. A quadrilateral has four sides. It also has four corners. Count the number of sides on each figure. The only choice that does not have four sides is choice D. It has five sides. It is a pentagon.

1 Which plane figure has three sides and three corners?

A rhombus **C** square

B triangle **D** hexagon

2 Kasey drew this picture.

Which plane figure is ***not*** in this picture?

A hexagon

B pentagon

C quadrilateral

D triangle

3 How many corners does a hexagon have?

A 3 **C** 5

B 4 **D** 6

4 What is the name of this figure?

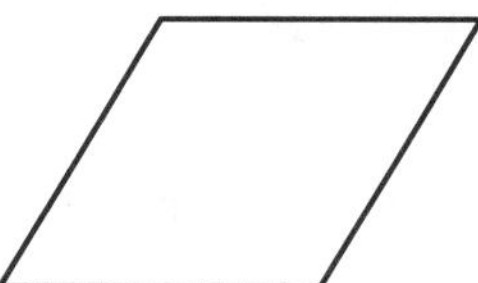

A rhombus **C** square

B rectangle **D** triangle

5 What is the name of a plane figure with five sides?

A hexagon

B pentagon

C rectangle

D rhombus

6 How many corners does a rectangle have?

A 2 **C** 4

B 3 **D** 5

Read each problem. Write your answer.

SAMPLE A plane figure has four sides that are all the same length. It has four corners. What is the name of the plane figure?

Answer ______________________

The plane figure is a rhombus. A rhombus has four sides that are the same length. It also has four corners. The corners are not always square. A square also has four equal sides. It always has square corners. The problem does not say if the corners are square. This figure must be a rhombus. It might be a square, but you cannot tell for sure.

7 Draw a plane figure with three sides and three angles in the space at the right. Name the figure.

Answer ______________________

8 Look at the two plane figures below.

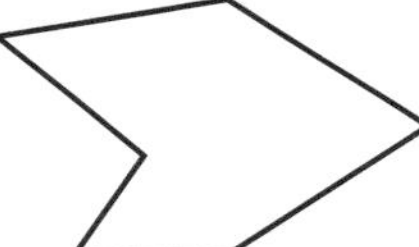

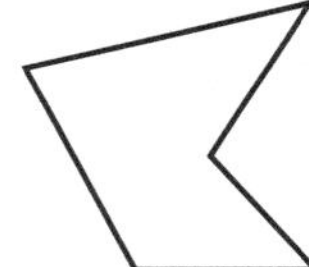

Circle the hexagon. Put an X on the pentagon.

9 Draw a plane figure with four sides and four corners in the space at the right. Make the opposite sides the same length. Make all the corners squares. What are two names for this plane figure?

Answer ____

Read the problem. Write your answer to each part.

10 Marta and Yukiko are making posters. Their posters are plane figures. Marta's poster has three sides and three angles. Yukiko's poster has five sides and five angles.

Part A Draw the shape of Marta's poster. Draw the shape of Yukiko's poster. What are the names of these shapes?

Marta's poster **Yukiko's poster**

____________________ ____________________

Part B Joe also made a poster. His poster is a plane figure. It has four sides and four angles. What is the name of this plane figure? Explain how you know.

What is the name for ***all*** plane figures with four sides and four angles?

____

____

____

____

Lesson 2

Solid Figures

2.G.1

A **solid figure** is not flat. Some solids can stand up by themselves. Some solids can roll. Solid figures have special names.

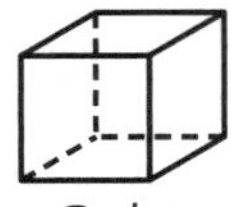
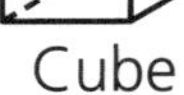
Cube

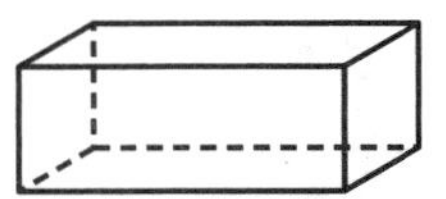
Rectangular prism

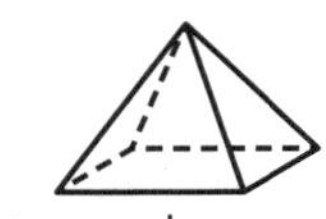
Rectangular pyramid

Solid figures have faces, vertices, and edges. Some solid figures have faces that are plane figures.

How many faces, vertices, and edges does this solid have?

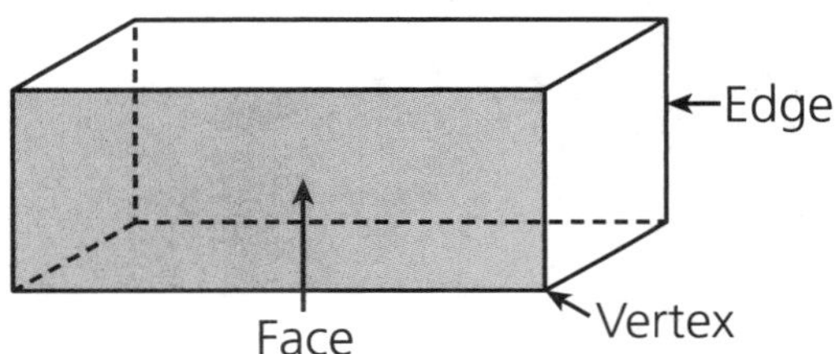

This solid is a rectangular prism. It has six faces. The faces are all rectangles. It has eight vertices. It has 12 edges.

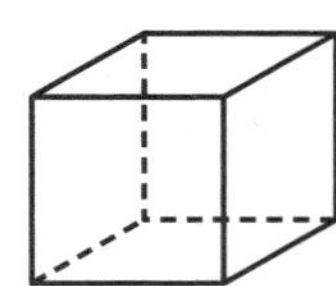

A **cube** is a kind of rectangular prism. It has six faces that are all squares.

Here are some other solid figures:

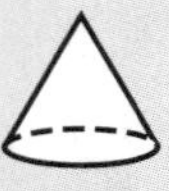
Cone

Cylinder

Sphere

Faces are the sides and bases of solids.

Edges are where the faces meet.

Vertices are the corners where the edges meet. *Vertices* is the word for more than one **vertex.**

Read each problem. Circle the letter of the best answer.

SAMPLE Which solid figure has six faces that are the same size?

A cube **C** rectangular pyramid

B square **D** cone

The correct answer is A. A square is not a solid figure, so choice B is not correct. A cube is a type of rectangular prism. A rectangular prism always has six faces. A cube always has six faces that are all squares. The squares are all the same size.

1 Which of these is a rectangular prism?

A  **C** 

B  **D** 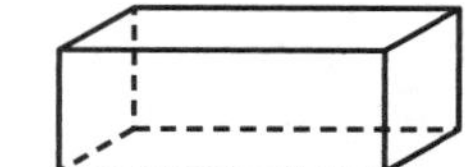

2 What is the name of the figure shown below?

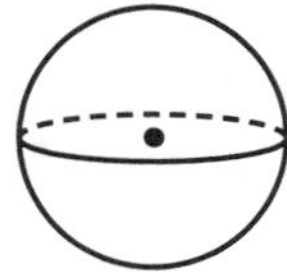

A cone **C** cylinder

B sphere **D** cube

3 Which of these is a cube?

A 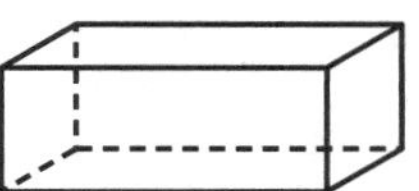 **C** 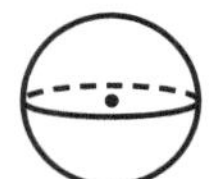

B  **D** 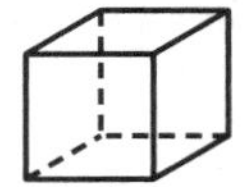

4 This solid figure is a rectangular pyramid.

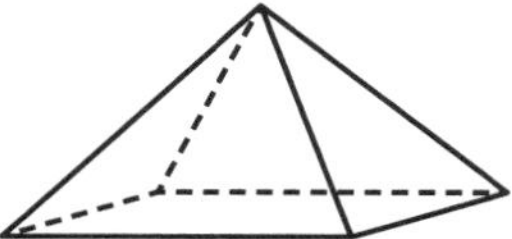

How many vertices does the rectangular pyramid have?

A 4 **C** 6

B 5 **D** 7

5 Look at the figure below.

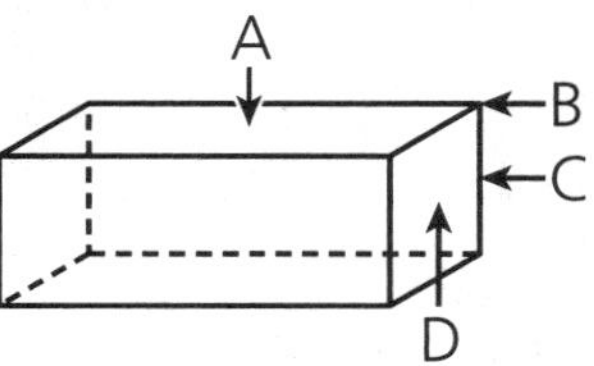

Which arrow points to an edge of the solid figure?

A arrow A **C** arrow C

B arrow B **D** arrow D

Read each problem. Write your answer.

SAMPLE Look at this solid figure.

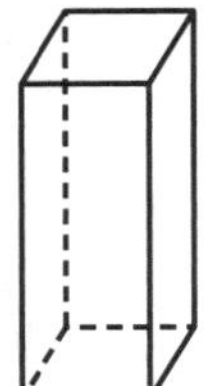

How many faces does this solid figure have?

Answer __________

This solid figure has six faces. The figure is a rectangular prism. Count the faces of the rectangular prism. The faces are the sides and the base of the figure. There are six faces.

6 A cube is a solid figure. It has six faces that are all the size. What plane figure always forms the sides of a cube? Draw the plane figure in the space at the right.

Answer ____________________

7 Look at the solid figure below.

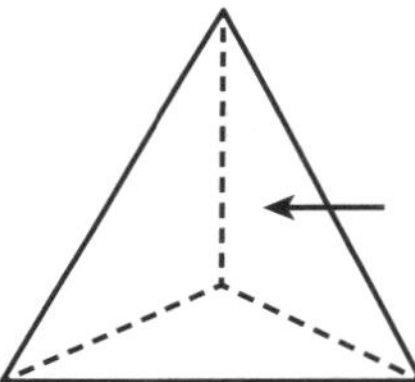

What is the shape of the face the arrow is pointing to?

Answer ____________________

8 What is the name of the solid figure shown below?

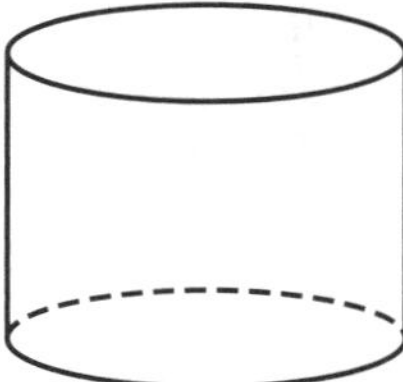

Answer ____________________

Read the problem. Write your answer to each part.

9 Oliver has a building block. The building block is shaped like a cube.

Part A Draw Oliver's building block in the space below.

Part B Is a cube also a rectangular prism? Explain how you know.

What plane figure is each face of a cube? What plane figures are the faces of a rectangular prism?

Lesson 3 Area

2.G.2

The space inside a rectangle is called **area.** You can measure area with square units.

The squares are all the same size. They are equal units. They sit side by side.

Different rectangles can have the same area.

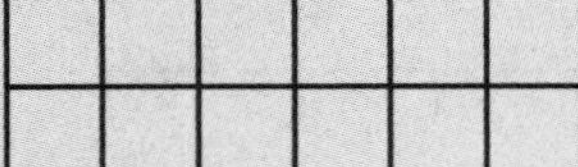

This rectangle has 2 rows of 6 squares. It has an area of 12 square units.

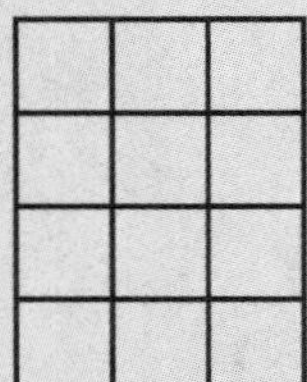

This rectangle has 4 rows of 3 squares. It has an area of 12 square units.

You can divide a plane figure into smaller pieces. This is called **partitioning.**

You can partition a rectangle into rows of equal squares.

How many squares fill this rectangle?

Divide the rectangle into squares that are the same size, like this: □

Make rows of squares. Each row has the same number of squares.

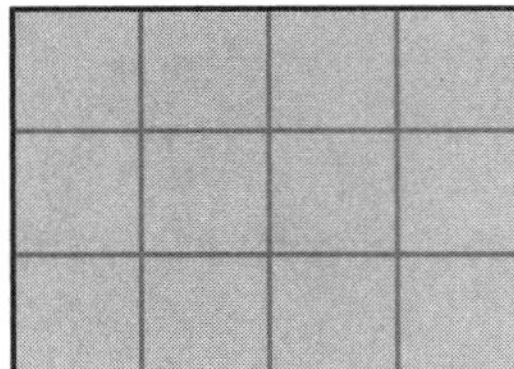

Count the number of squares.

This rectangle has 3 rows of 4 squares. There are 12 squares in all.

The space inside this rectangle is 12 square units.

Read each problem. Circle the letter of the best answer.

SAMPLE Look at the rectangle below.

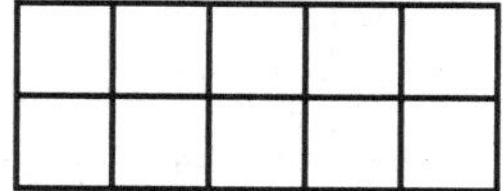

How many squares are inside this rectangle?

A 5 **B** 10 **C** 12 **D** 15

The correct answer is B. Count the squares in the top row. There are 5 squares. Count the squares in the bottom row. There are 5 squares. Add: 5 + 5 = 10. There are 10 squares in all.

1 Which rectangle is partitioned into 6 squares?

A

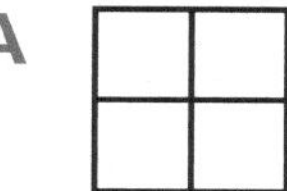

C

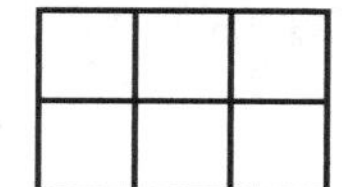

B

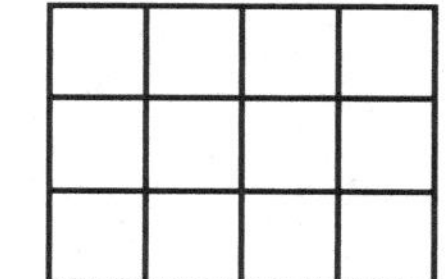

D

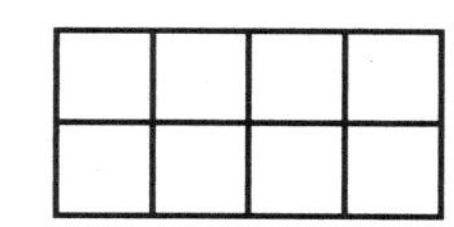

2 How many squares are inside this rectangle?

A 4 **C** 16

B 5 **D** 20

3 Look at this rectangle.

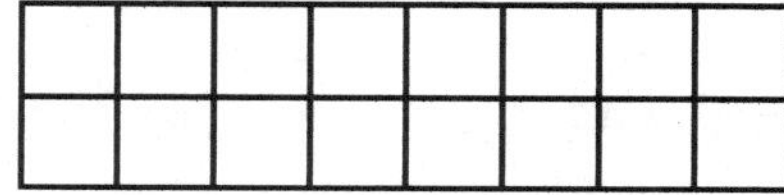

Which rectangle has the same number of squares?

A

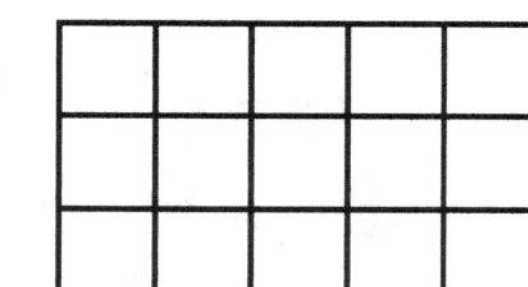

B

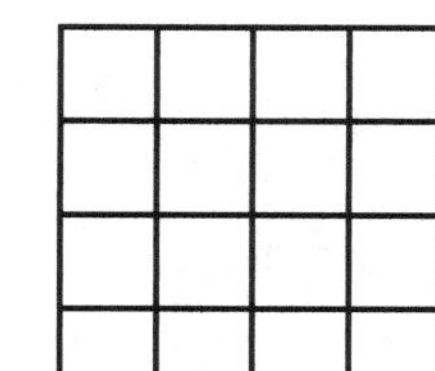

C

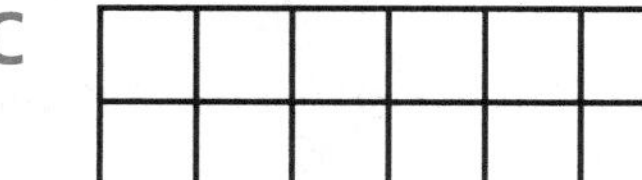

D

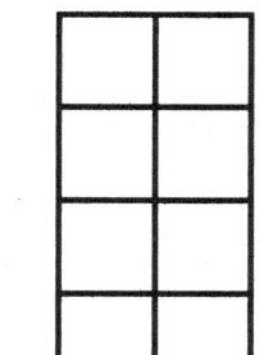

Read each problem. Write your answer.

SAMPLE Look at this rectangle.

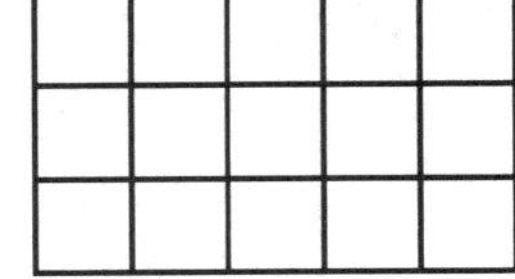

Andrea says a rectangle with 5 rows of 3 squares is the same size. Is Andrea correct? Explain.

Answer ______________________________

Yes, Andrea is correct. This rectangle has 3 rows of 5 squares. Count by 5's to find the total: 5 + 5 + 5 = 15 squares. Count to find how many squares in a rectangle with 5 rows of 3: 3 + 3 + 3 + 3 + 3 = 15. The rectangles have the same number of squares.

4 Partition the rectangle below into 4 rows of 6 squares.

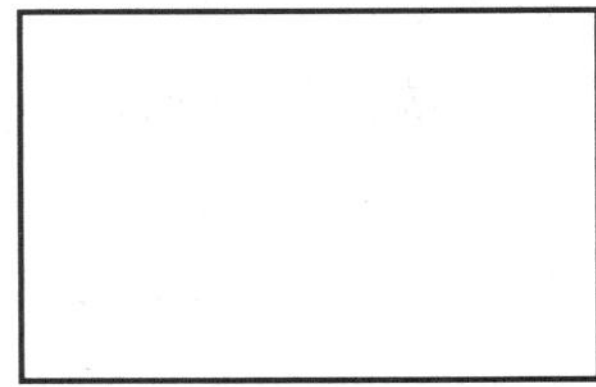

How many squares are there in all?

Answer __________

5 Hector builds a rectangle with 3 rows of 6 squares. Jill builds a rectangle with the same number of squares. Jill's rectangle has a different number of rows.

What could Jill's rectangle look like? Draw it below.

Read the problem. Write your answer to each part.

6 Keane wants to draw a rectangle that is 20 squares in size.

How many equal rows of squares add to 20?

Part A Show two different ways Keane can draw a rectangle of this size.

Part B Explain how you know the rectangles are the same size.

____

____

____

____

Lesson 4

Partitioning Shapes

2.G.3

Equal-sized pieces have the same shape and size.

A circle is a type of plane figure. It does not have any sides or corners.

Use these words to show partitioning:

Half
Third
Fourth

You can partition shapes in different ways.

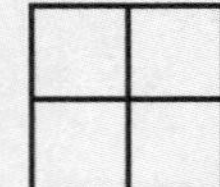

This shows fourths.

This also shows fourths.

You can partition, or divide, a plane figure into smaller pieces. The pieces should all be the same size.

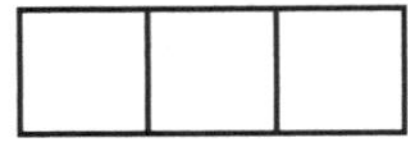

This is correct. This is not correct.

A plane figure can be divided into two, three, or four equal parts. These parts have names.

How many parts is this circle divided into?

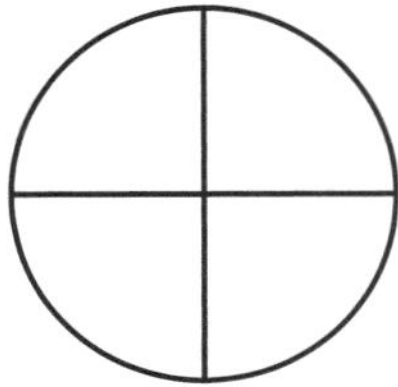

This circle is divided into four smaller parts. It is divided into fourths.

The whole circle equals four fourths. Each piece is one-fourth.

How many parts is this rectangle divided into?

This rectangle is divided into two smaller parts. It is divided into halves.

The whole rectangle is two halves. Each piece is one-half.

Read each problem. Circle the letter of the best answer.

SAMPLE Which figure shows thirds?

A 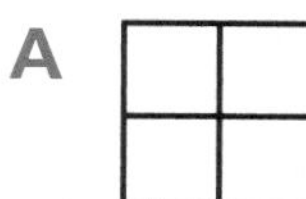 B C D 

The correct answer is B. The word *thirds* means "three equal parts." Choices A and D show four parts. They are not correct. Choices B and C show three parts. Only choice B has equal parts.

1 What word describes the pieces of this circle?

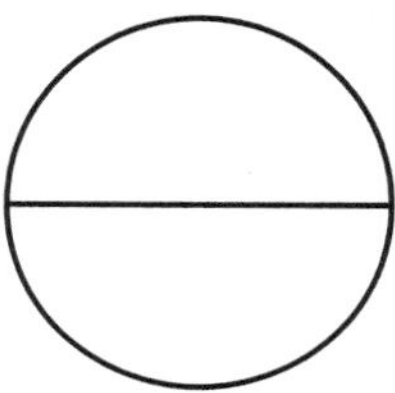

A halves **C** fourths

B thirds **D** squares

2 Zoe divided a square into fourths. How many equal parts did it have?

A 1 **C** 3

B 2 **D** 4

3 Which rectangle is ***not*** divided into thirds?

A 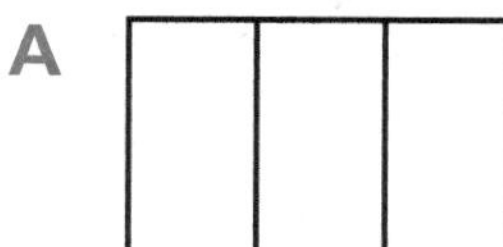 **C** 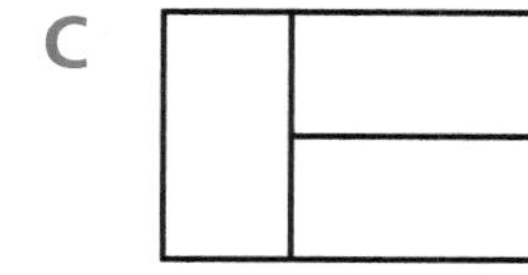

B 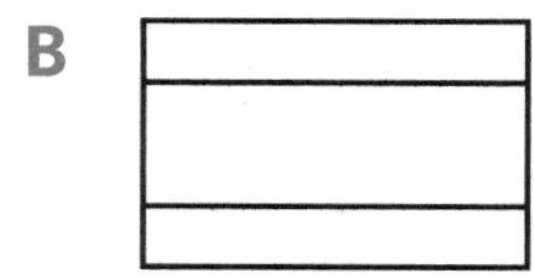 **D** 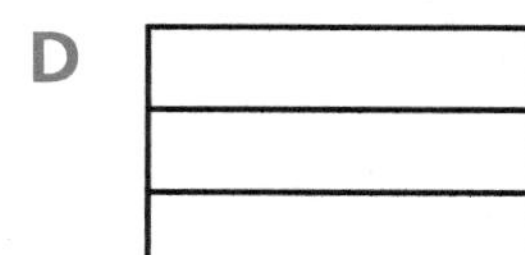

4 Which shows a circle partitioned into fourths?

A **C** 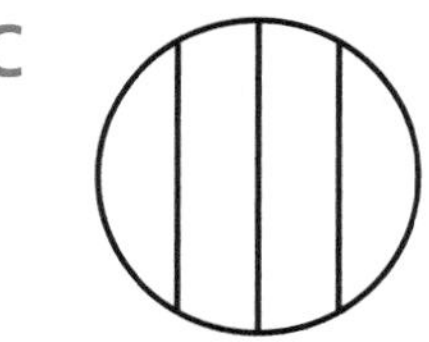

B  **D** 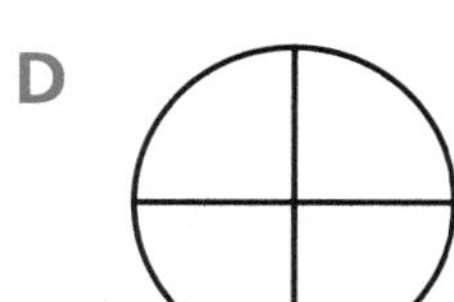

Read each problem. Write your answer.

SAMPLE What words describe one piece of this circle?

Answer ______________________________

One piece of this circle is *one-third* of the circle. The circle is partitioned into three pieces. The pieces are all the same size. The circle is partitioned into thirds. So one piece is one-third of the circle.

5 Atil divided this circle as shown here.

What part did he divide it into?

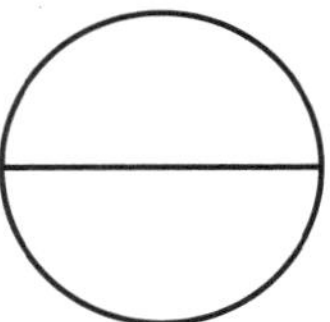

Answer ____________________

6 Partition this square into fourths.

7 Heather divided this rectangle. She says she made thirds.

Is Heather correct? Explain how you know.

____

____

Read the problem. Write your answer to each part.

8 The rectangles below are the same size.

Part A Partition both rectangles into halves. Show two different ways to partition the rectangles.

Part B How many halves make up a whole rectangle? Explain how you know.

How can you draw lines on the rectangles to make equal shares?

REVIEW

Geometry

Read each problem. Circle the letter of the best answer.

1 What is the name of this plane figure?

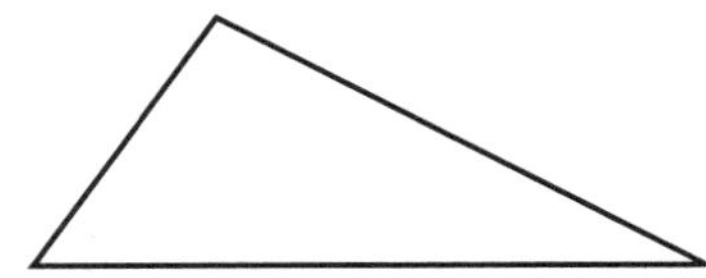

A rectangle
B square
C pentagon
D triangle

2 How many squares is this rectangle divided into?

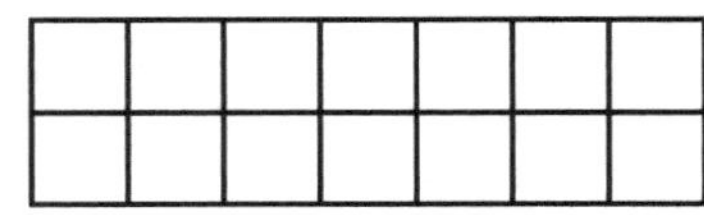

A 6
B 8
C 12
D 14

3 What is the name of this solid figure?

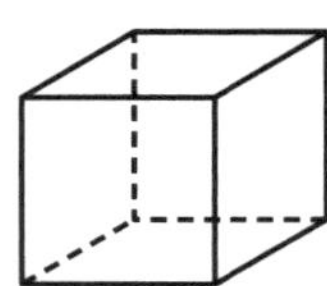

A cube
B cylinder
C square
D cone

4 Which of these shows the rectangle divided into fourths?

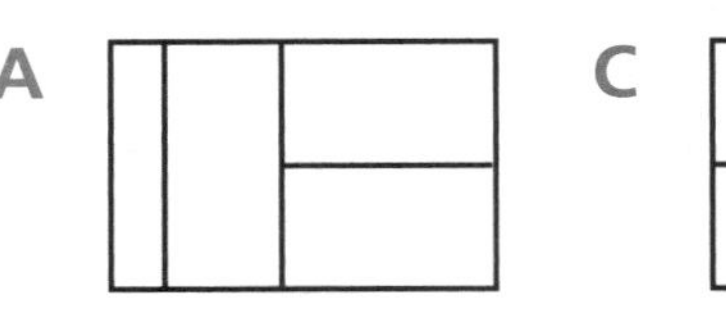

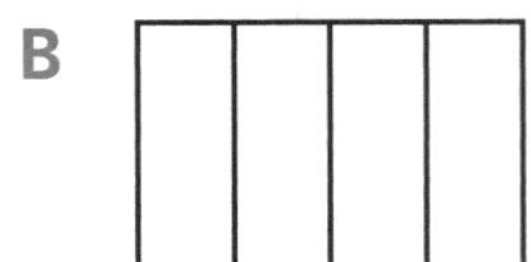

A, B, C, D

5 Which plane figure has six sides and six corners?

A hexagon
B pentagon
C rhombus
D square

6 The solid figure below is a rectangular pyramid.

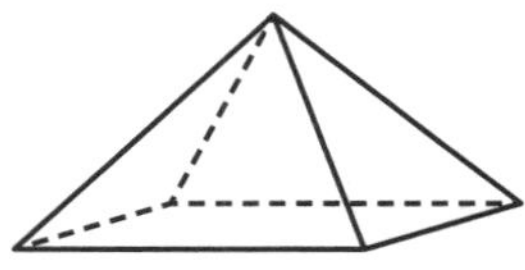

How many edges does this solid figure have?

A 5
B 6
C 8
D 10

Read each problem. Write your answer.

7 Divide this circle into three equal pieces. What word describes the pieces?

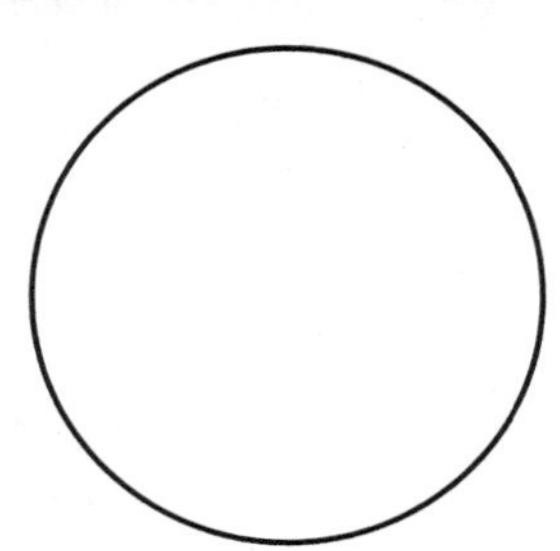

Answer ____________________

8 Look at the plane figures below.

What name fits both of these plane figures?

Answer ____

9 How many faces does a cube have?

Answer __________

10 Partition the rectangle below into 3 rows of 8 squares.

How many squares are there in all?

Answer __________

11 Draw a triangle in the space at the right.

Read the problem. Write your answer to each part.

12 Nadia is cutting plane figures out of paper. She cuts out a plane figure. It has five sides and five corners.

Part A Draw Nadia's plane figure in the space below. What is the name of this plane figure?

Answer ____________________

Part B Nadia cut out another plane figure. It has four sides. The opposite sides are the same length. It has square corners. What plane figure did Nadia cut out? Explain how you know.

____

____

____

____

PRACTICE TEST

Read each problem. Circle the letter of the best answer.

1 Pam invited 38 people to a party. Only 23 people could come. Which number sentence could you use to find how many people could ***not*** come?

A 38 + 23 = ☐

B 23 − 38 = ☐

C 38 − ☐ = 23

D 38 + ☐ = 23

2 Haley skip counted by 5's. She started at 0. She ended at 20. Which shows the numbers she said?

A 0, 10, 20

B 0, 5, 10, 15, 20

C 0, 2, 4, 6, 8, 10, 12, 14, 16, 18, 20

D 10, 15, 20

3 Find the sum.

$$\begin{array}{r} 12 \\ 54 \\ 18 \\ +14 \\ \hline \end{array}$$

A 84 **C** 94

B 88 **D** 98

4 Logan washed his car. What is a good estimate for the length of the car?

A 4 inches **C** 12 inches

B 4 feet **D** 12 feet

5 What is 10 more than 587?

A 588 **C** 597

B 577 **D** 687

6 Tasha found three one-dollar bills, five quarters, and one dime in her purse. How much money did Tasha find?

A $4.40 **C** $4.10

B $4.35 **D** $3.35

7 Which of these will have an even number as a sum?

A 9 + 9 **C** 8 + 1

B 3 + 4 **D** 7 + 6

Read each problem. Circle the letter of the best answer.

8 What symbol goes in the box to make a correct comparison?

185 ☐ 183

A $<$　　**C** $=$

B $>$　　**D** $+$

9 This picture graph shows how many marbles Koji has.

KOJI'S MARBLES

Color	Number
Blue	○○○○
Red	○○○○○○○
Green	○○○○○

Key: ○ = 2 marbles

How many red marbles does Koji have?

A 4　　**C** 10

B 7　　**D** 14

10 Add:

$$\begin{array}{r} 42 \\ +35 \\ \hline \end{array}$$

A 67　　**C** 83

B 77　　**D** 87

11 What is the name of the figure shown below?

A triangle　　**C** rhombus

B pentagon　　**D** rectangle

12 A school office has these mailboxes for the teachers.

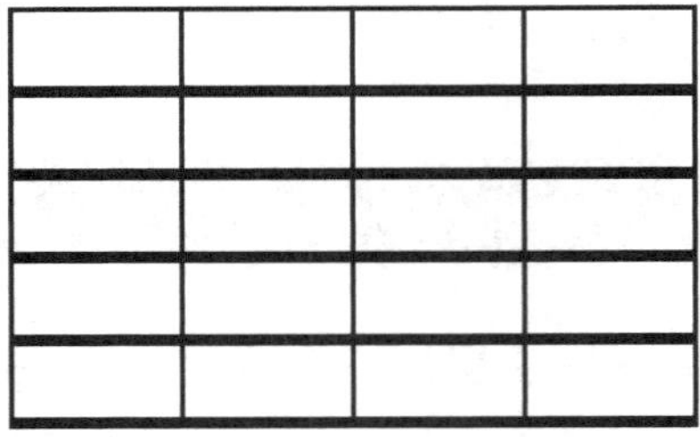

How many mailboxes are there in all?

A 10　　**C** 20

B 16　　**D** 24

13 What is 924 written with words?

A nine hundred twenty-four

B nine two four

C ninety-two and four

D nine hundred two four

14 Julia has piano lessons in the afternoon. Her lesson starts at the time shown on the clock.

What time does Julia's lesson start?

A 3:20 A.M.　　**C** 3:20 P.M.

B 4:15 A.M.　　**D** 4:15 P.M.

Read each problem. Circle the letter of the best answer.

15 Use your centimeter ruler to help you answer this question.

What is the length of this pushpin?

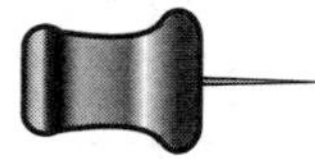

A 1 centimeter

B 2 centimeters

C 3 centimeters

D 4 centimeters

16 Look at the circle below.

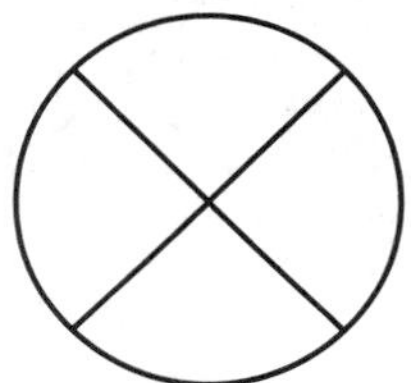

Which describes one piece of the circle?

A one-fourth

B one-third

C one-half

D one whole

17 How many tens are in a hundred?

A 1 C 10

B 5 D 100

18 This rectangle has been partitioned into same-size squares.

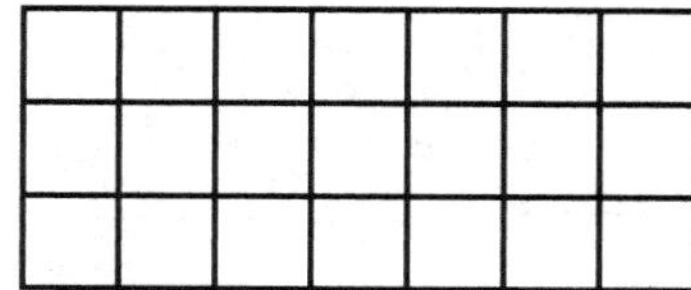

How many same-size squares are in this rectangle?

A 7 C 20

B 10 D 21

19 Jim collected 257 cans to recycle. Beth collected 308 cans. How many cans did Jim and Beth collect in all?

A 555 C 565

B 556 D 566

20 Noah needs a chain that is 50 feet long. He has a chain that is 36 feet long. How much more chain does Noah need?

A 14 feet C 24 feet

B 16 feet D 26 feet

Read each problem. Circle the letter of the best answer.

21 Use your inch ruler to help you answer this question.

How long is this toy car?

A 1 inch
C 3 inches
B 2 inches
D 4 inches

22 Gabby measured each window in her house. She made this line plot to show the heights.

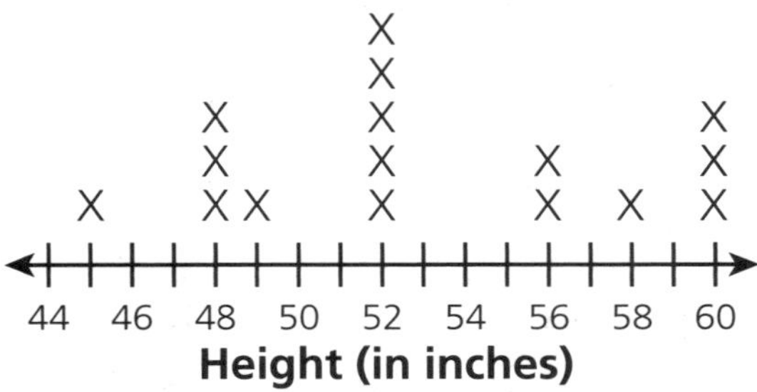

Which height were the greatest number of windows?

A 48 inches
C 56 inches
B 52 inches
D 60 inches

23 There are two benches beside a soccer field. One bench is 96 inches long. The other bench is 72 inches long. The team pushes the benches together to make one bench. How long is this bench?

A 72 inches
C 166 inches
B 96 inches
D 168 inches

24 A zoo has 3 elephants and 8 lions. It has 9 tigers and 4 giraffes. Which bar graph correctly shows this data?

A
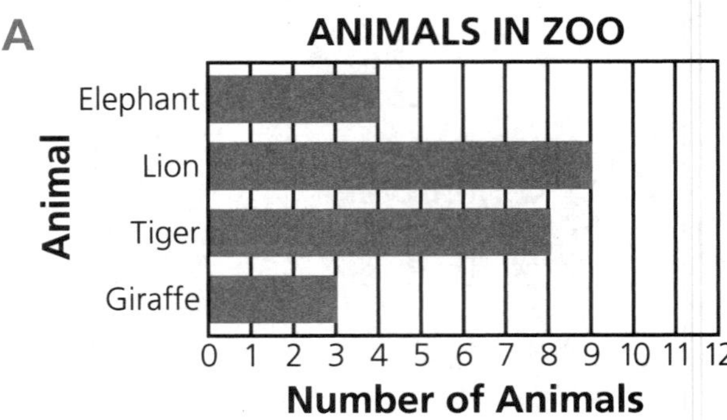

B
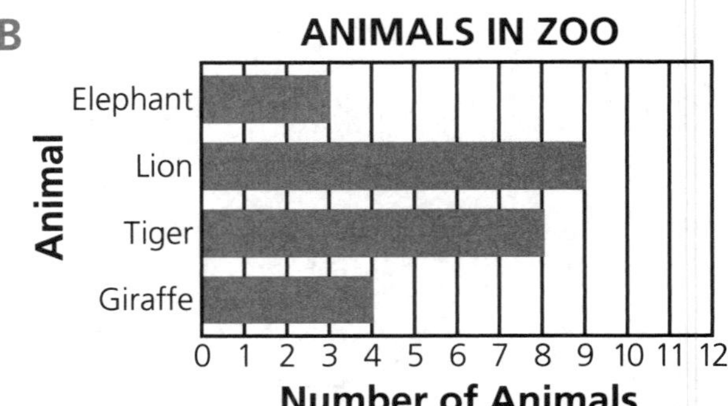

C
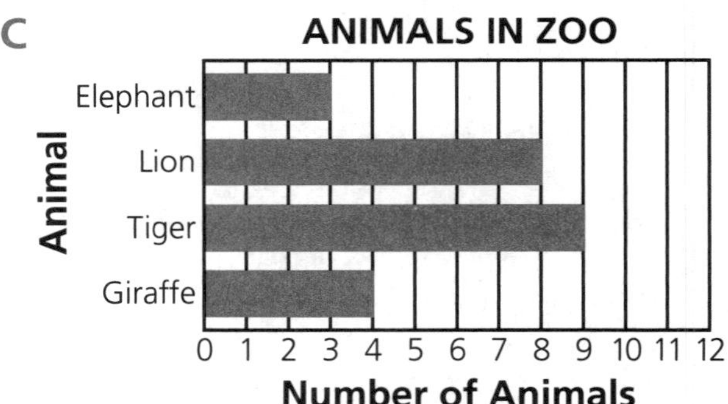

D
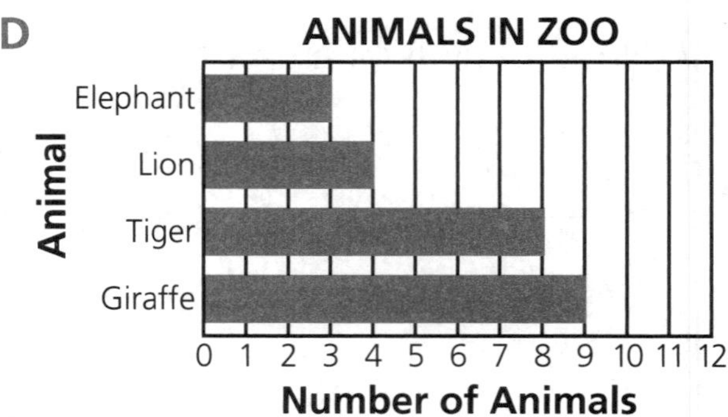

Read each problem. Circle the letter of the best answer.

25 What is the sum of 9 and 3?

A 6

B 10

C 11

D 12

26 Which is the same as 600?

A 6 hundreds, 0 tens, 0 ones

B 6 hundreds, 10 tens, 0 ones

C 6 hundreds, 10 tens, 10 ones

D 6 hundreds, 100 tens, 10 ones

27 Use your centimeter ruler to help you answer this question.

Rae has these two bolts.

A 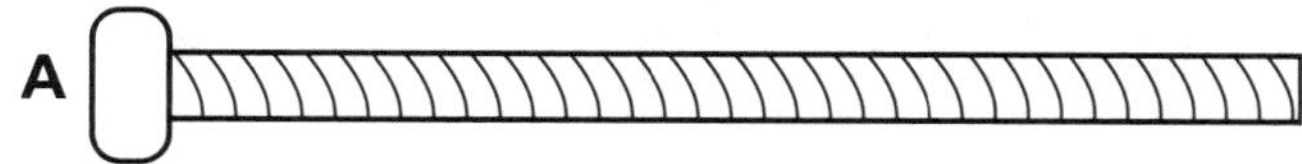

B 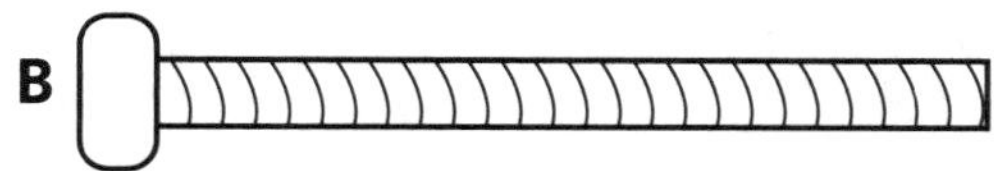

How much longer is bolt A than bolt B?

A 1 centimeter

B 2 centimeters

C 3 centimeters

D 4 centimeters

28 Which number is 4 hundreds, 9 tens, and 2 ones?

A 249

B 294

C 429

D 492

29 Which of the following shows a cube?

A

C 

B

D 

30 Which number line shows point *B* 35 units from 0?

A 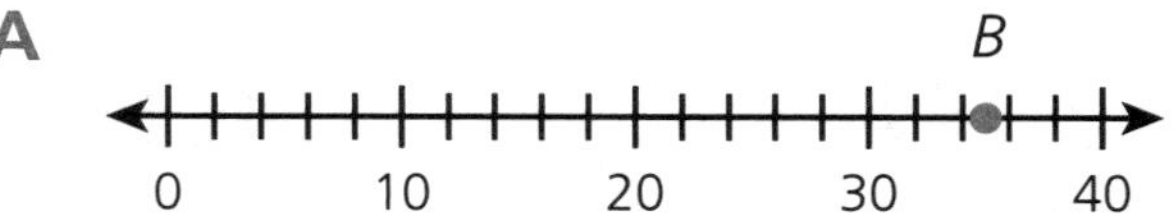

B 

C 

D 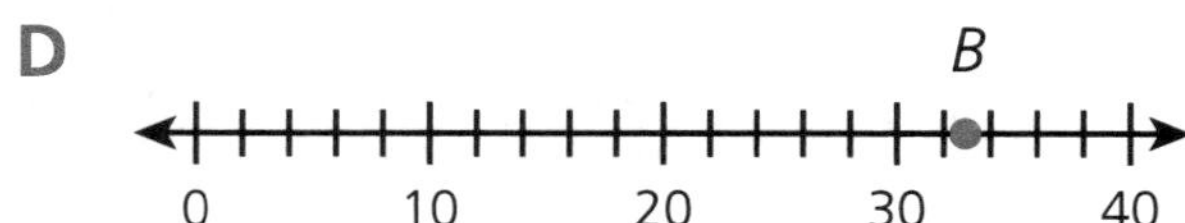

Read each problem. Write your answer.

31 Mrs. O'Connell wrote this number on the board.

736

Write the number of hundreds, tens, and ones in this number.

Hundreds __________

Tens __________

Ones __________

32 Use your inch ruler to help you answer this question.

How long is the feather below?

Answer ____________________

33 Ten students each threw a ball. They measured how far they had thrown the ball. The distances, in feet, were 12, 13, 13, 15, 18, 18, 18, 19, 20, and 20. Make a line plot to show this data.

Read each problem. Write your answer.

34 What is the expanded form of the number 307?

Answer ______________________

35 Antonio left school at half past 2. Draw hands on the clock to show this time. Write the time on the digital clock.

36 Destiny bought 14 apples and 21 oranges. She and her family ate 15 pieces of fruit. How many pieces of fruit were left? Show your work.

Answer ___________

37 Look at the set of squares below.

Is the number of squares even or odd? Explain how you can tell without counting.

____

____

____

Read each problem. Write your answer.

38 Skip count from 300 to 400 by 10's. Write the numbers you would say.

Answer ______________________________

39 Partition the rectangle below into 4 rows of 5 squares. How many squares are in the rectangle in all?

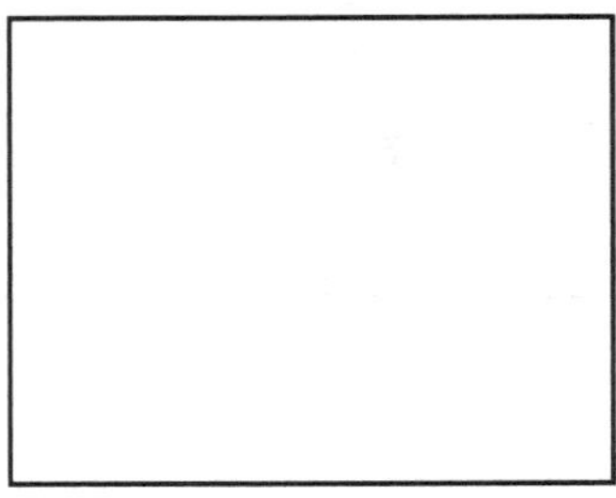

Answer __________

40 Use your centimeter ruler to help you answer this question.

Katya has two pieces of ribbon.

A 

B 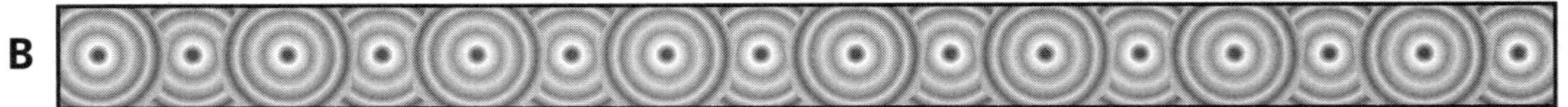

How much longer is ribbon B than ribbon A?

Answer ____________________

41 Subtract 46 − 12. Use the number line to find the difference.

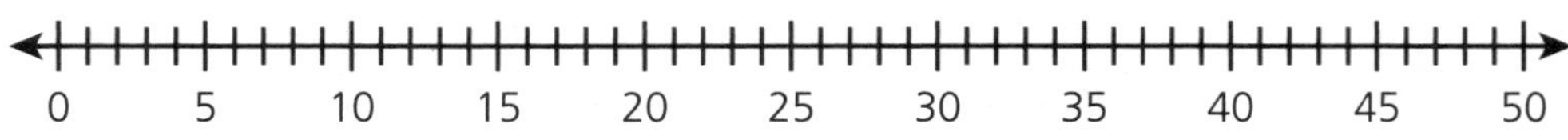

Answer __________

Read each problem. Write your answer.

42 Find the difference. Show your work.

$$\begin{array}{r} 72 \\ -56 \\ \hline \end{array}$$

Answer ___________

43 What basic fact can you use to subtract 850 − 200?

Answer ______________________

44 Ivan drew a plane figure. It had five corners. Draw Ivan's figure. What is the name of Ivan's figure?

Answer __________________________________

45 Subtract 17 − 8 in your head.

Answer ___________

Read each problem. Write your answer.

46 Cassie measured a stick with an inch ruler. It was 9 inches long. Tim measured the same stick with a centimeter ruler. It was 23 centimeters long. Explain why Cassie and Tim did not get the same measurement.

47 Explain how to subtract 299 from 434.

Read each problem. Write your answer.

48 The picture on the right shows the money in Hans's right pocket. The picture on the left shows the money in his left pocket.

Left pocket

Right pocket

How much money does Hans have in all?

Answer ____________________

49 Steve has 256 baseball cards. Jawon has 265 baseball cards. Compare the number of baseball cards. Use >, <, or =.

Answer ______________________________

50 Divide this rectangle into thirds. How many thirds are in the rectangle?

Answer __________

Read the problem. Write your answer to each part.

51 One morning, 473 people came into a store. In the afternoon, 516 people came into the store.

Part A How many more people came into the store in the afternoon than in the morning? Show your work.

Answer ___________

Part B Explain how you could use place-value blocks to help you do this problem.

____

____

____

____

____

Read the problem. Write your answer to each part.

52 A second-grade class voted on their favorite recess activity. The table below shows the results.

FAVORITE RECESS ACTIVITY

Activity	Number of Votes
Tag	8
Jump ropes	3
Kickball	7
Swings	4

Part A Make a bar graph to show this data. Remember to label your bar graph and give it a title.

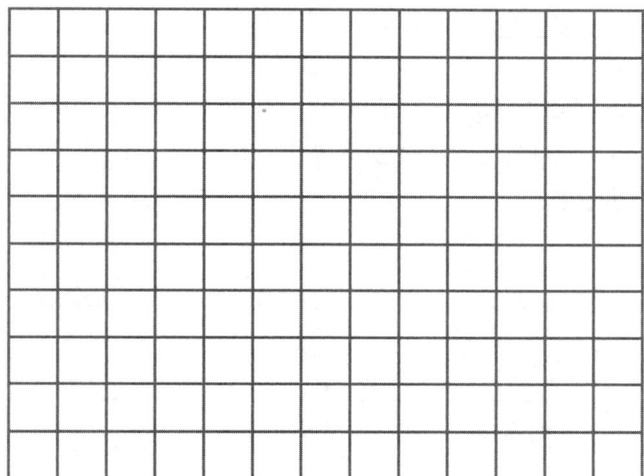

Part B How can you tell which is the most popular activity by looking at the bar graph? Explain your answer.

____

____

____

____

Read the problem. Write your answer to each part.

53 Amanda drew a plane figure. It had four sides and four corners. All the sides were the same length. All the corners were square corners.

Part A Draw Amanda's plane figure below. What is the name of this plane figure?

Answer ____________________

Part B Amanda drew another plane figure. It also had four sides and four corners. Is it the same as the first figure? Explain your answer.

____

____

____

____

____

____

GLOSSARY

A

add to combine numbers

area the space inside a plane figure

B

bar graph a display that shows data by using bars

C

centimeter a small unit of length in the metric system; 100 centimeters = 1 meter

centimeter ruler a ruler marked in centimeters

clock a tool used to tell time

compare to decide which number is greater than or less than another number

count to name numbers in order to find a total

cube a solid figure with six square faces

customary system the measurement system used mostly in the United States; measures length in inches and feet

D

data information

decompose to break a number apart

difference the answer in a subtraction problem

digit a numeral from 0 to 9

doubles facts addition facts where both addends are the same; example: $4 + 4 = 8$

E

edge the place where two faces meet in a solid figure

equal having the same value

equation a number sentence with an equals sign (=) that says two things have the same value

estimate to make a good guess

even numbers numbers that end in 0, 2, 4, 6, or 8

expanded form a number written as the sum of its places; example: $200 + 30 + 5$ is the expanded form of 235

F

face the side or base of a solid figure

fact family four related number sentences that use the same three numbers

foot a medium unit of length in the customary system equal to 12 inches; plural *feet*

height how tall something is

hexagon a plane figure with six sides and six corners

hundreds the third place from the right in a number; example: the 2 in 235 is in the hundreds place

inch a small unit of length in the customary system

inch ruler a ruler marked in inches

key the part of a pictograph that tells the value of each symbol

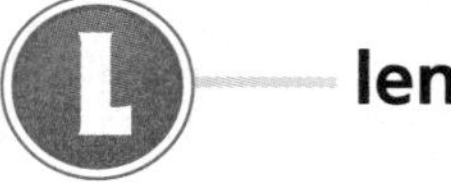

length how long something is

line plot a display that shows data with X's and a number line

measure to find the size of something

meter a large unit of length in the metric system equal to 100 centimeters

metric system the measurement system used in most countries; measures length in centimeters and meters

money bills and coins used to pay for things

N

non-standard unit a unit of measurement that is not always the same; example: paper clips and fingers

number chart a chart showing numbers from 1 to 100 in rows of 10

number line a line showing numbers in order from least to greatest

number sentence a group of numbers and operation symbols that shows something about numbers

O

odd numbers numbers that end in 1, 3, 5, 7, or 9

ones the first place on the right in a number; example: the 5 in 235 is in the ones place

parallelogram a quadrilateral with opposite sides that are the same length

partitioning dividing a plane figure into smaller pieces

pentagon a plane figure with five sides and five corners

pictograph a display that shows data by using symbols or pictures

placeholder the digit 0 used in a number to show there is no value in a certain place

place value the value of a digit in a number

plane figure a flat shape

point a place on a number line

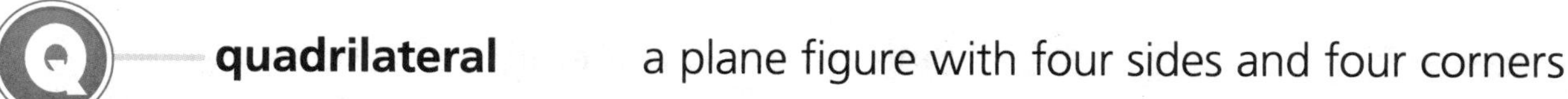

Q

quadrilateral a plane figure with four sides and four corners

R

rectangle a quadrilateral with opposite sides that are the same length and square corners

regroup to change the value of a digit to the place value to the left or right; example: 1 ten = 10 ones

rhombus a quadrilateral with four sides that are the same length

ruler a tool used to measure length

S

scale numbers along the side or across the bottom of a graph

skip count to count without saying every number

solid figure a shape that is not flat

square a rectangle with four sides that are the same length

standard form a number written with digits in place values

standard unit a unit of measurement that is always the same; example: inches and centimeters

strategies ways to do something

subtract to take a number away from another number

sum the answer in an addition problem

tens the second place from the right in a number; example: the 3 in 235 is in the tens place

triangle a plane figure with three sides and three corners

vertex the corner where edges meet in a solid figure; plural *vertices*

whole numbers numbers used to count and zero (0, 1, 2, 3, …)

width how wide something is

word problems number stories

plus sign

equal sign

greater than symbol

less than symbol

rectangle

triangle

rhombus

square

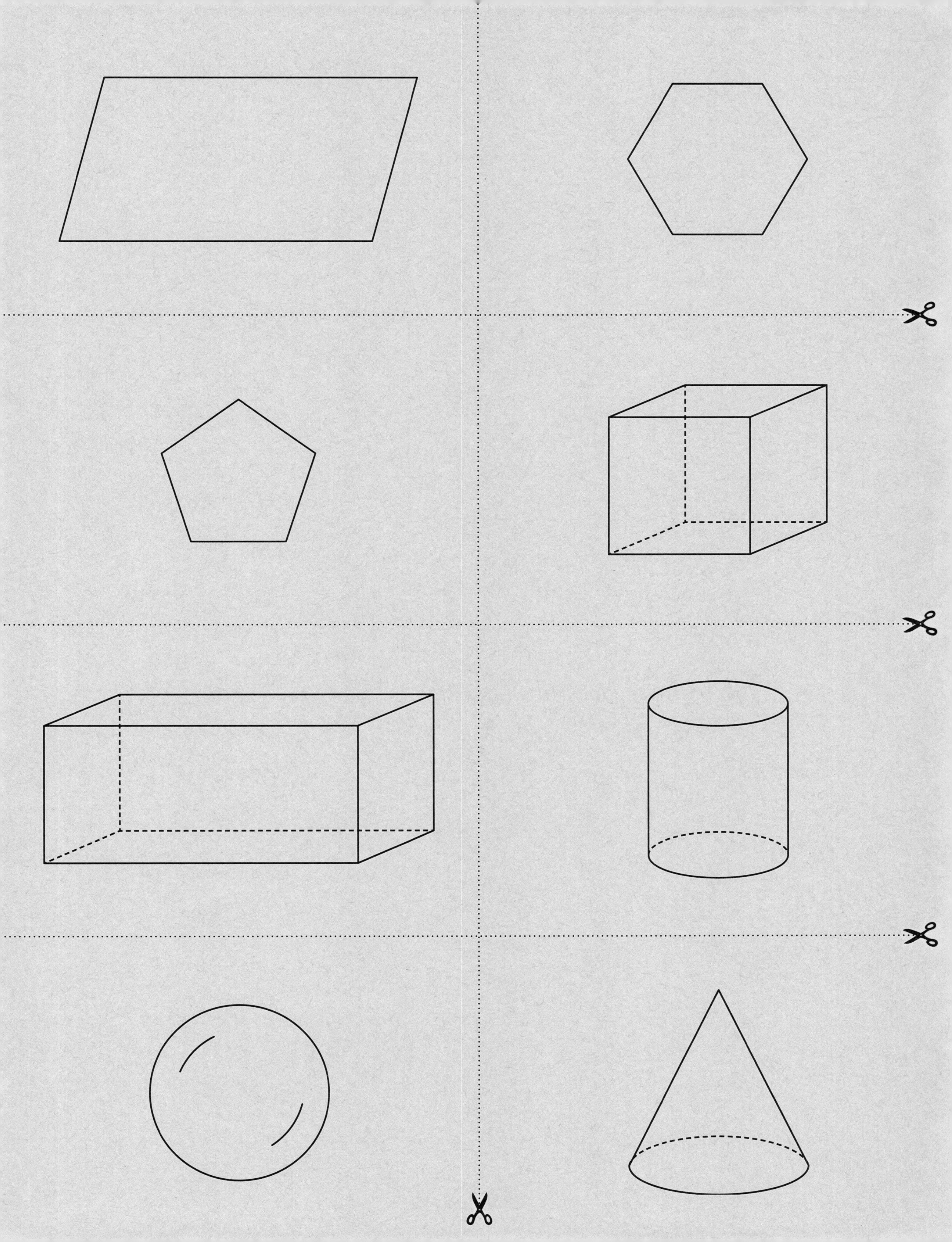

hexagon	parallelogram
cube	pentagon
cylinder	rectangular prism
cone	sphere

$-$

$2 + 2 = 4$

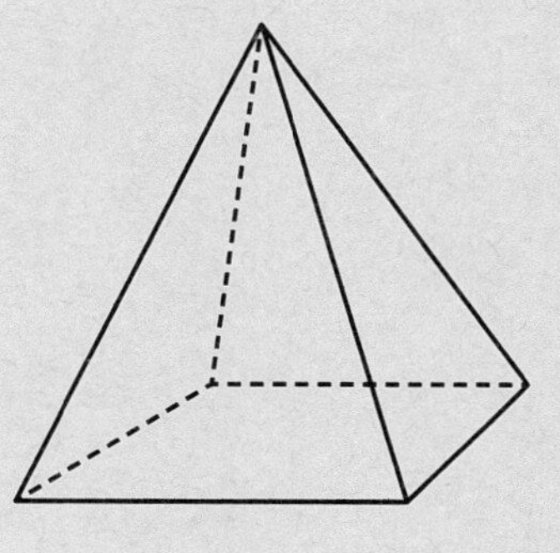

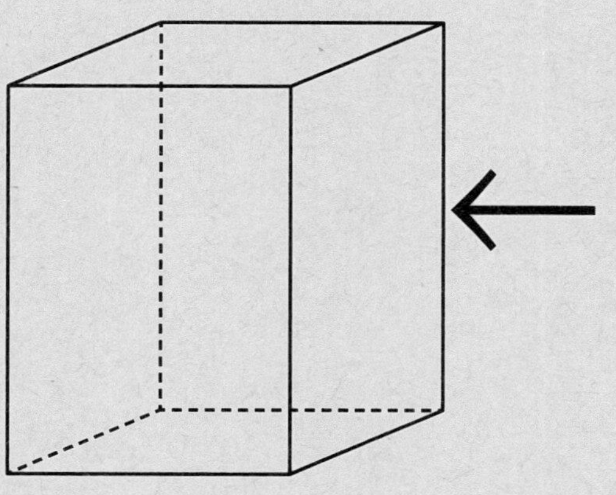

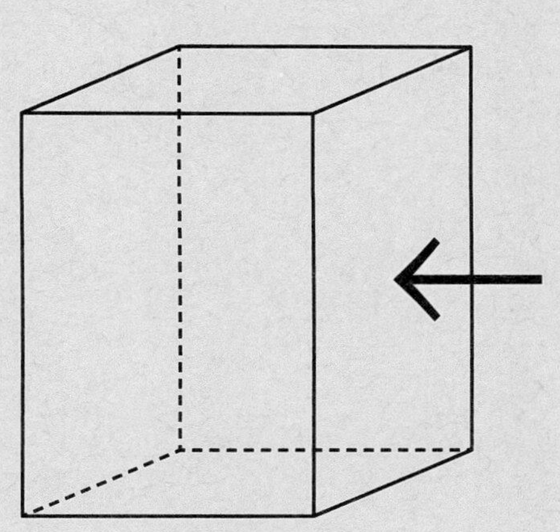

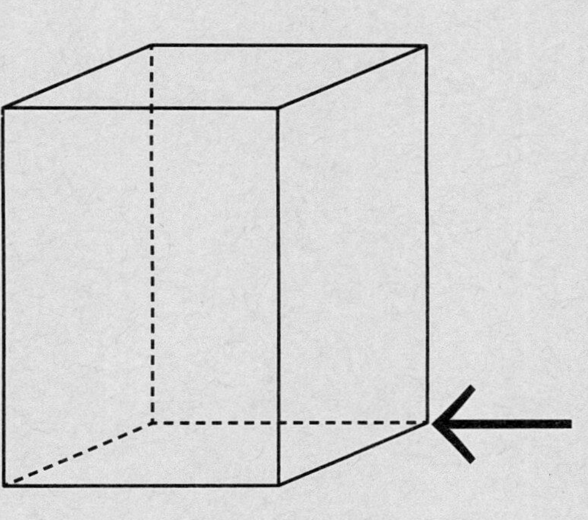

sum

minus sign

hour hand

minute hand

edge

rectangular pyramid

vertex

face